Serve It Up

Serve It Up

Volleyball for Life

WILLIAM NEVILLE
University of Washington

MAYFIELD PUBLISHING COMPANY

Mountain View, California
London • Toronto

Library of Congress Cataloging-in-Publication Data

Neville, William.
    Serve it up : volleyball for life / William Neville.
        p.   cm.
    Includes index.
    ISBN 1-55934-110-6
        1. Volleyball.   I. Title.
    GV1015.3.N48   1993
    796.325—dc20

                                                        93-36096
                                                        CIP

Manufactured in the United States of America
10   9   8   7   6   5   4   3   2   1

Mayfield Publishing Company
1280 Villa Street
Mountain View, California 94041

Sponsoring editor, Erin Mulligan; production editor, Lynn Rabin Bauer; manuscript editor, Andrea McCarrick; text and cover designer, Richard Kharibian; cover photographer: Rod Searcey; art editor, Jean Mailander; illustrators, Willa Bower, Cyndie C. H. Wooley, and Wayne S. Clark; manufacturing manager, Martha Branch. The text was set in 10/12 Times New Roman by Thompson Type and printed on 50# Butte des Morts by Banta Company.

 This book is printed on recycled paper.

To Inspire the Youth within Us Forever:

"I would rather be ashes than dust! I would rather that my spark should burn out in a brilliant blaze than it should be stifled by dry rot. I would rather be a superb meteor, every atom in me a magnificent glow, than a sleepy, permanent planet. The proper function of man is to live, not to exist. I shall not waste my days in trying to prolong them. I shall use my time."

—Jack London

Contents

Preface

The game presented here is volleyball. It is a game that can be played in a huge variety of ways. It can be incredibly complex or pea-brain simple. To this unbiased, objective, discriminate author, volleyball is the perfect game. It can be played for life, by all people, at all levels, indoors, outdoors, with any number of people. Sometimes you don't need a ball or a net or a court (just don't forget the people). It provides maximum and/or minimum physical exertion, depending on the chosen intensity level. And it has colorful jargon, a lexicon that will make you sound like a world-class player even though your only chance of "heating one up" is over a ping-pong net. But after all is said and done, it's fun, just plain fun.

The purpose of this book is to share how to execute, practice, and apply the skills that make playing volleyball fun. The text sets students up for success by providing an introduction to the mechanics of each skill and information about mental preparation, strategies, and game application. To help students hone skills, included within each chapter are troubleshooting tips, and at the back of the book you'll find perforated, fill-in-the-blank skill worksheets. A complete chapter on physical training will expose students to a fitness program that will help them to develop the strength and stamina to enjoy volleyball and prevent injuries. Chapters on tournament play and varieties of volleyball equip students with fun and practical information to help them continue playing and/or coaching volleyball for the rest of their lives. As a bonus, the text is a how to talk volleyball primer. The ultimate goal, of course, is to convince you that playing volleyball makes the world a better place. Simple.

I would like to thank the following reviewers for their useful suggestions about the revision of the manuscript: Barbara Drum, University of Maryland at College Park; Karen Fredenburg, Baylor University; Brenda Gray, Sam Houston State University; Dixie Grimmett, California State University, Long Beach; Harriet Henry, Buena Vista College; Rhonda McMullen, Metro State College of Denver; Debbie Masten, Northeast Missouri State University; Charles Raynor, North Carolina State University; Russell Rose, Pennsylvania State University; and Robert Zorn, Arizona State University.

Introduction

Welcome to the great game of volleyball! You are about to learn an activity that will provide a lifetime of enjoyment. Volleyball will provide opportunities for physical fitness, an outlet for competitive urges, social exchange, intellectual challenge, and endless hours of fun. Volleyball never gets dull. Not only is the nature of the game spontaneous, the varieties of formats and venues make it adaptable to virtually any situation.

The objective of this book is to provide easily understood information and guidance in learning the skills and tactics of volleyball. Many varieties of the game are included to illustrate how and where to participate. The information contained herein should be as applicable to the casual player as to the most competitive hard case.

This book has an underlying theme: Volleyball is meant to be *played*. Although it is true that the better your skills can be executed the more joy you will have playing, the focus is on playing rather than perfect execution. Often, sports are taught with precise performance in mind, with application to the game being a secondary purpose. There is also the teaching method of just "roll out the ball and let them play." This book, however, aims to provide information leading to efficient skill performance while learning how to play.

Finally, a book on volleyball should be enjoyable to read. If a goal is to promote the fun of the game, then it follows that the presentation should be informative but light. At the end of most chapters you will be encouraged to stop reading about volleyball and go out and *do it!* Also, there will be the occasional piece of sage advice to add to your philosophy of action. So, let's roll!

Mintonette to Volleyball: A Brief History

1

In 1895, the businessmen in Holyoke, Massachusetts, were getting edgy about their physical condition during the winter months. Basketball was in its early development but required bathing after a game, cutting into midday exercise time. Throughout the history of the Young Men's Christian Association (YMCA), program and physical education directors have been notably creative in developing programs to serve the needs of the public. William G. Morgan, physical director of the Holyoke YMCA, identified a need and created a game: mintonette. He strung a badminton net (probably inspiring the original name) 6 feet off the center of a basketball floor. He took the bladder out of either a soccer or basketball. The game's competitive objective was simple: Put the ball down on the opponent's floor while keeping it off your own. There was no limit to the number of players or contacts.

Mintonette was played by innings like baseball. The activity's objective was some exercise without much sweat, thus reducing bathing time. Little did Morgan know what he had hatched. Several months after the introduction of mintonette, Springfield College Professor Alfred T. Halstead convinced Mr. Morgan to change the name to volleyball because it was more descriptive and marketable to a sports-minded public.

EVOLUTION OF THE EARLY GAME

Between 1897 and 1900, volleyball's popularity grew. The Spaulding Company developed the first official volleyball. A basketball and soccer ball were too heavy and their bladders too light. The first official rules were written, requiring the use of the Spaulding ball and raising the net to 7 feet. The YMCA was the main promoter of the game.

During 1912 and 1913, the rules were revised, creating the basic premise of the game as it is today. Ball-handling technique and related violations were standardized. The net was raised once again, to 7½ feet. Rotation of players was introduced, which became the signature of volleyball. The intent was to minimize specialization by requiring all players to perform all the skills. Games were to 21 points. In 1913, the YMCA introduced volleyball to the world at the Far East Games in Manila, where it was an official event.

During World War I, American forces introduced the game to Europe, passing out 16,000 Spaulding volleyballs. The net was raised to 8 feet, and 2-out-of-3-game matches replaced 21-point games.

VOLLEYBALL AS A CHAMPIONSHIP GAME

In 1922, the Brooklyn, New York, YMCA won the first national championship held at the YMCA of Pittsburgh, Pennsylvania. Pittsburgh was also the site of the first scholastic volleyball program, developed by C. Lawrence Walsh and Harry Batchelor in 1924. Again the rules were revised to restrict contacts to three per side before the ball had to be sent over the net. The ball could be touched only above the waist. The court dimensions were restricted to a 35-by-60-foot playing area.

The United States Volleyball Association (USVBA) was organized in 1928 at the Yale Club in New York for the purpose of representing volleyball nationally and internationally and conducting an annual national men's championship. Women and girls were not yet given the opportunity to play volleyball. Also in 1928, the first collegiate program was created at Oregon State College, and the plans for conference play were in the works.

Competitive volleyball became more sophisticated throughout Europe during World War II. American troops played the game casually and recreationally, but the Europeans recognized the competitive potential. In 1947, the Federation Internationale de Volley-ball (FIVB) was founded to organize international competition and standardize rules worldwide. The big, powerful Soviet men's national team beat an equally sizable crew from Czechoslovakia in the inaugural World Championship in 1949 in Prague.

It is stunning that women did not play volleyball officially for 54 years. However, in 1949, Houston's women's volleyball team, the Eagles, strode away with the first USVBA National Open Women's Championship held in Los Angeles. The first women's World Championship was won by the Soviets in Moscow in 1952. The U.S. did not field a team.

As the competitive demands increased during the 1950s and 1960s, great changes and an improvement in techniques and strategies occurred. Two basic schools of thought emerged: (1) the European methods emphasized power, size, and in-your-face brute force; and (2) the Japanese countered the inherent European size with complex offensive patterns, deception, quickness, and precise ball control. The confrontation of these styles over the years led to the creation of many varieties. The U.S. was not a world power over these years, despite fielding teams of outstanding athletes. The U.S. teams were all-star squads, yet they had limited training time together, poor funding, and little international experience. Occasionally, a U.S. team upset one of the international powers; however, the highly organized, funded, and trained juggernauts from Europe and Asia were winning most of the international tournaments.

In 1964, men's and women's volleyball were introduced as official events at the Tokyo Olympic Games. A few years later, in 1969, the National Association for Intercollegiate Athletics (NAIA) held its first collegiate championship for men. The Division for Girls and Women's Sports also held its first national championship this year. The National Collegiate Athletic Association (NCAA) followed suit in 1970. The USVBA had a collegiate division in its national championships since the 1950s.

VOLLEYBALL IN THE U.S.

The 1970s might have been the decade that had the most influence on U.S. volleyball. Even though the U.S. won the Olympics and World Championships in the 1980s, the groundwork had been laid in the previous decade. The FIVB began a serious effort to develop youth and junior volleyball through something called "mini volleyball." In 1975, the USVBA created the first full-time training center near Houston, Texas, for the women's national team, and the men followed suit with a center in Dayton, Ohio, in 1976. These were the first attempts to have the national teams train in one place. Also in 1975, the Federal statute Title IX was passed, requiring equal extracurricular opportunities for girls and women in federally funded institutions. Volleyball became a major scholastic sport for girls and women in high schools and colleges and, thus, increased the need for professional, full-time coaches. The Association for Intercollegiate Athletics for Women (AIAW) parlayed Title IX into full-time coaching positions and college scholarships for the first time in 1975.

In 1981, the NCAA recognized the growth of women's volleyball and created the first "final four" for collegiate women. The AIAW was absorbed by the NCAA, standardizing recruiting and scholarship rules for men and women. Also in 1981, the U.S. men's full-time national team training center moved to San Diego to prepare for the 1984 Olympic Games. The team was ranked nineteenth in the world. Meanwhile, the more established U.S. women's team was training in Orange County, California.

After years of intense training, the U.S. women captured the silver medal in the 1984 Los Angeles Olympics and the men won the gold. The U.S. had emerged as a major force in international volleyball and solidified its reputation with gold-medal efforts in the 1985 World Cup, 1986 World Championship, and 1988 Seoul Olympics. Both U.S. teams continue in full-time training programs and are always in medal contention.

VOLLEYBALL TODAY

In recent years, professional volleyball in Europe has offered million-dollar contracts, expanding the opportunities for elite players. Professional beach volleyball has exploded around the world, led by the Association of Volleyball Professionals (AVP), which has cultivated major sponsorship dollars and promotion. The FIVB is aggressively promoting the beach phenomenon. Four-person men's and women's teams playing outdoors in professional leagues has also met with success. The USVBA's youth and junior program has created outstanding opportunities for young people to develop their skills and play at a high level. The FIVB World League, which organizes selected countries into divisions, offers millions of dollars in prize money annually.

There are countless people and anecdotes that make up the history of volleyball and give a perspective on the future of this great game. However, despite the glamour the game has received in recent years, William G. Morgan's invention has the same benefits today as it did in 1895: it fosters friendships, provides great fun, has few facility and equipment requirements, and, unless one is playing at a highly competitive level, reduces the need for a bath after playing.

Basic Facilities, Equipment, and Rules

2

As volleyball has developed, so has the equipment. Entrepreneurs have recognized the growth of volleyball as a gold mine. However, no one needs to spend much money to play the game.

FACILITIES

Playing six-person volleyball indoors requires a court 18 meters long by 9 meters wide surrounded by a clear area of at least 2 meters (Figure 2.1). All lines on a volleyball court are 5 centimeters wide. Court dimensions are measured from the

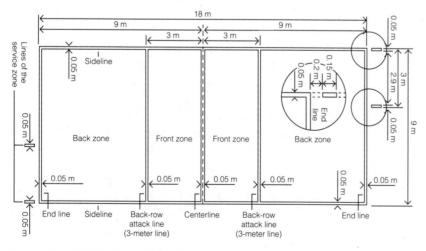

Figure 2.1   Volleyball court dimensions

outside edge of the lines. There is a centerline with the net directly above it. In addition, there are two lines, one on each half-court 3 meters back from the centerline. These lines are known as the 3-meter lines, or back-row attack lines. The service area on each half of the court is measured from the right sideline as you face the net 3 meters along the end line and marked with 15-by-5-centimeter lines. The playing area should be well lit and have a minimum height of 7 meters (23 feet) to the lowest obstacle hanging from the ceiling; however, it is strongly recommended to have at least 30 feet of overhead clearance.

EQUIPMENT

Nets and Poles

There is a wide range of nets and poles available today. Safety is the most important criterion for selecting equipment. The net poles need to be the kind that can be sunk directly into built-in receptacles in the floor. *Poles with weighted bases and support guy wires are extremely dangerous.* There should be no obstacles or protrusions around the net supports. Sports Imports of Columbus, Ohio, supplies the top-of-the-line poles and net systems called Senoh (see Appendix B). The net should have a metal cable or a recently developed synthetic cable in the top to ensure the proper tension (Figure 2.2). If you use a cabled net, make sure to tape the burrs of steel that will emerge after several uses so that players won't get sliced during net setup or play. The net also needs nylon "piggin strings" to secure the net to the poles after the cable and a rope the length of the bottom of the net have been tightened. This centers the net in relation to the court. Two antennae are attached to the net, one extending above the net over each sideline. The antennae should be securely fastened to the top and bottom of the net so that they cannot become dislodged during the course of play. Antennae are available through companies that sell poles and nets.

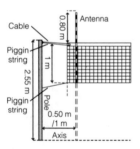

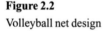

Figure 2.2
Volleyball net design

Balls

Playing with a good ball may be the difference between having fun and seeking another recreational activity. Play with a quality ball. The ball needs to be laceless, round (and stay round), and constructed of at least 12 panels (18 is best) covering an air-filled bladder. The circumference must be between 62 and 68 centimeters (25 to 27 inches) and weigh between 260 and 280 grams (9 to 10 ounces). There are many good balls on the market, as well as poor ones. Avoid synthetic (as in "fake") leather. Baden Sports, an American company, makes a top-of-the-line indoor ball that is durable, keeps its roundness over time, and is easy to play with (see Appendix B).

Clothing

If you play indoors for recreational purposes, a T-shirt and shorts are perfect. You can play in sweatpants, but you will probably rip out the knees. A good pair of knee pads are preferable to save the knees in groveling floor defensive play. Some people prefer to play in long-sleeve shirts to cushion hard-hit shots to the forearms or to absorb moisture so that the ball won't slip on contact. The most important piece of apparel is a good pair of shoes. Regardless of your level of play, the strain on the feet is constant. A high-quality pair of volleyball shoes will save your feet and make the experience more enjoyable. As in all athletic shoe markets, volleyball shoe sales are very competitive. Nike makes a superb shoe, among others.

If you play competitive volleyball, there are specific uniform guidelines, including colors, size of numbers, and other adornments. These will be thoroughly explained by the team and/or league in which you play. Outdoor volleyball emphasizes comfort in apparel with virtually no limitations beyond those governed by indecent-exposure laws.

BASIC RULES

There are several organizations that write volleyball rules. The rules accepted worldwide are the International Volleyball Rules written by the Rules of the Game Commission of the FIVB. However, in the United States there are several sports organizations that write their own rules to fit what they believe are the best interests of their programs. The U.S. is the only country in the world that does not universally accept FIVB rules. Fortunately, in most cases the differences are relatively minuscule and getting closer all the time. What follows is a general overview of the salient rules.

Number of Players

Traditional volleyball is played with two teams of six players of the same sex on the court at one time. There can be substitutes. The number of subs and times they can enter the game vary in different sets of rules. Volleyball can be played with teams of doubles, threes, and fours, indoors or outdoors, and with players of both sexes.

Height of Net

The universal net heights are 2.24 meters (7 feet 4⅛ inches) for women and 2.43 meters (7 feet 11⅝ inches) for men and coed players. In the U.S., elementary schools set the net at 1.85 meters (6 feet 1 inch) for both girls and boys.

Points and Games

A *game* of volleyball (internationally called a *set*) consists of 15 points, with the winning team having to win by 2 points. For example, a team leading 15 to 14 must score again to win. International rules have added a 17-point cap, meaning that the first team to score 17 wins, regardless of whether the opponent has 16 points. In some U.S. organizations, there is no cap. A *match* normally consists of a team winning 3 out of 5 games. However in the U.S., tournaments can consist of 2-out-of-3-game matches in the interest of time. A *point* can be scored only when a team is serving. A team that wins a rally when receiving the serve gains the right to serve; this is known as a *sideout*. **Exception:** International rules and many U.S. organizations require a *rally point* scoring system in the final and deciding game of a match (5th in the best of 5, 3rd in the best of 3). A point is scored on every rally regardless of who is serving. There is no 17-point cap.

Rotation

After each change of serve, the team winning the serve must *rotate*. That is, each player must move to the next adjacent court position in a clockwise direction and be in that position when the serve is contacted. The positions are numbered 1 through 6 in a counterclockwise direction, beginning with right back as position 1, right front as position 2, middle front as position 3, and so on.

One of the most important but confusing rules in volleyball is *overlap*. A player's feet cannot be beyond an adjacent player. For example, the middle back player cannot be in front of the middle front player or to the sides of the right back or left back player. The left back player cannot be to the right of the middle back player or in front of the left front player. A clear understanding requires a walk-through on the court because there are legal overlaps. For example, the right back player can overlap the middle and left front players toward the net but not the adjacent right front player. Yikes. Study the rotation and overlap rules. They are important to the tactics and playing of volleyball.

Contacts

Each team gets no more than three legal contacts before it must send the ball back over the net. **Exception:** If the ball being attacked by the opponent is touched by a block attempt, it is not counted as one of the three allowable contacts. A *legal contact* is defined as the ball being hit without coming to a visible rest. (The violation known as a *lift* is called if the ball is hit after coming to a visible rest.) If more than one hand or arm is used, the hit must be simultaneous. There are some exceptions to these interpretations that can be found in the various rule books.

The Service Area and 3-Meter Line

The serve must be initiated from the service area, defined in the court dimensions in terms of a 3-meter area in width on the right side of the back line. However, the server can go back as far as the facility will allow in that 3-meter corridor. Also, a server attempting a jump serve must take off before the end line but can land inside the court as long as he or she contacts the ball before his or her feet touch the floor. If a player is in a backcourt rotational position (right, middle, or left back) he or she can attack the ball above the top plane of the net as long as he or she takes off from behind the 3-meter attack line. The player can land in front of the line as long as ball contact was completed before the feet touch down on the floor.

These are the basic rules defining the premise and intent of volleyball. For complete definitions, commentary, and interpretations of the rules you may contact the various rule governing bodies listed in Appendix B.

Learning the Skills

3

The quality of teaching depends on the simplicity of the method. Sometimes the subject matter is complicated. If the method of teaching is also complex or, even worse, dull, then the chance of successful learning is in doubt. This chapter describes the guidelines for learning the various skills presented in this book. Keep in mind that learning physical skills out of a book is virtually impossible. Simple activities are presented to enhance the skill-acquisition process; however, you must clearly understand the importance of active involvement in gamelike activities to master the skills.

EFFICIENT LEARNING

There is continual research and related debate on the most efficient ways to teach and learn. Virtually everyone agrees that one must "do it" to really learn a skill. The debate rages about progressions (part–whole method) versus whole method only with attention to keys and block learning (mechanical repetitions) versus random learning (the selected skill emphasized within the context of a gamelike situation as it naturally occurs). If a person does something long enough, often enough, he or she will learn that skill, regardless of the methodology. The question is what is the most efficient way of learning. Whole-method execution of a skill with attention to specific keys in gamelike activities is presented here. Random learning will be a priority, because an essential ability to *play,* is to be able to call up the correct motor program the instant the situation dictates it.

To get good at it, practice it. If you learn each skill by rote you may learn the mechanics quicker but will have difficulty applying them in games, where reactions, anticipation, adaptability, and adjustments pay high dividends. You want to become a player not a clinic demonstrator. Certainly rote, or block, learning has a place in troubleshooting and in mechanics introduction, but the faster techniques can be applied to the game, the faster you will learn to play. This will also lengthen your retention of playing ability.

The sequence for quality learning is:

1. Modeling the skill with attention to the first key.
2. Engaging in opportunities to respond (activities that practice the skill).
3. Getting feedback, with attention to the demonstrated key.

This sequence is continued until all mechanical keys are covered. Then the practice activities are based around gamelike drills. Learning begins with modeling, is consummated by providing many opportunities to respond, and is supported by offering feedback based on the keys. The skills are presented in the same sequence as they occur in a game. Some coaches teach the skills in an arbitrary order of importance. This presentation is designed around the premise that learning volleyball should be as gamelike as possible, hence the normal sequence.

The skills will be presented in the following format:

1. A description of the skill.
2. A description of the skill's application in the game.
3. Learning keys and principles (where appropriate).
4. Specific tactics unique to the skill.
5. "Go do!" activities (drills that focus on mechanics mastery).
6. A worksheet to easily organize and evaluate your learning regimen, found at the back of the book.

Serve

4

Serving is the skill used to put the ball in play. It is the only skill in volleyball for which the player has exclusive rights to the control of the ball. Every other skill relies on a rebound of the ball from one player to another. The player who serves gets to hold on to the ball, then initiate and control every movement related to serving. It is important for every player to understand this unique fact of volleyball: The server can duplicate exactly the same movements each time when serving the ball. All other skills require a reaction and adjustment to the ball and the dynamic conditions of the game.

There are three basic ingredients in the serving recipe:

1. *Mechanics.* As stated above, the mechanics of the serve can be exactly duplicated each time because there are no outside physical variables. There are several types of serves, each requiring somewhat different mechanics, but each serve is the same in itself.

2. *Mental preparation.* Aha! The art of serving can get its due. The thoughts that go through your mind prior to the physical expression of serving make you a tough server. Every time you practice serving, practice the mental process, reviewing exactly what you are going to do. Often on competitive teams, serving gets little focused attention. It is a relatively easy physical skill. Make it a habit to do it right every time.

   Effective servers are consistent mechanically, but more importantly they have a great ability to always hit a serve that is difficult to pass because it either has good velocity and movement, is targeted to a susceptible opponent, or hit to a glaring weak spot on the court. These players only miss when they are trying a tough serve. They are not timid and always concentrate on what their serve will do to their opponent.

3. *Game application.* Having mastered the mechanics of serving and the ability to concentrate, you should be able to make the most effective choice of target, placement, and velocity. Each time you are about to serve, review the tactical information gleaned from one or more of the following sources:

game plan based on scouting reports, the opponent's rotational order to which you are serving, the game situation when it is your serve, and opposing players who have either shown a lack of passing control or consistency during the course of the game. Finally, a nugget of knowledge: The most difficult area to receive serve is in the deep-left back corner because it requires the passer to move back and away from the target. Master a deep-line serve.

Serving is the easiest way for a player to apply tactics and learn more advanced tactical concepts. Mix these three ingredients together and you have an explosive formula. You can learn each of these elements almost simultaneously, even though the early focus will be on mechanics.

TYPES OF SERVES

There are several types of serves: the underhand float serve, the overhead, or "bow-and-arrow," float serve, the standing spike serve, the jump spin serve, the sky ball serve, the roundhouse, or "Asian," float serve, and the side spin, or "sidewinder," serve. The bow-and-arrow serve is the most common and consistently effective. It will be used as the primary example. However, the others will be referred to and their purposes described.

MECHANICS

Every serve has some basic elements and is governed by the same principles:

Elements
1. Ready position (Figure 4.1)
2. Toss/step (Figure 4.2)
3. Contact (Figure 4.3)

Figure 4.1   Serve ready position   **Figure 4.2**   Toss/step

Figure 4.3   Contact

Principles

1. In the ready position, prepare mentally—*review what you are going to do* with your serve (Figure 4.4).
2. Toss the ball in the *same place* every time.
3. Contact the ball *as high and as far in front of you* as can be controlled (Figure 4.5).
4. *See* your hand contact the ball.

Learning Keys

1. Ready position
2. Toss
3. Step
4. Hit

Figure 4.4   Mental preparation

Figure 4.5   High, forward contact

Figure 4.6 Ready position

The *ready position* is simple. For all serving skills, the weight should be mostly on the back foot. The lead foot should be pointed at the target with the lead leg comfortably flexed (Figure 4.6). The shelf arm is bent at the elbow, which is close to the body at approximately waist level. The ball is resting on the shelf hand in front of the body's centerline, with the horizontal panels facing the server. The hitting arm is held as if the server were about to pull a bow string (hence "bow-and-arrow" float), with the elbow bent and positioned at about eye level, comfortably away from the shoulder (see Figure 4.6). The wrist is firm and straight and will remain so throughout the serve. The hand, also firm and straight, points over the ball at the target. The eyes are glaring over the serving hand as if peering through a gun sight.

The "toss/step" is virtually completed in one, fluid motion. A *step* with the lead foot occurs at the same time the toss is being executed (Figure 4.7). The

Figure 4.7 Toss/step

Figure 4.8
Proper toss/step ball position

Figure 4.9
Contact

coordination of these two movements should look like there is a string attached from the tossing hand to the lead foot. If the ball were allowed to drop, it would land inside of and slightly in front of the lead foot's big toe (Figure 4.8). This step initiates the weight transfer. Some stronger players do not take a step but transfer the weight exclusively with the contact motion.

The *toss* is either the ignition of a serve's success or its demise. Make sure the toss is consistent every time. *Every time!* The toss is the beginning of what should be a compact motion. The tossing hand places the ball in the position where it will be contacted by the hitting hand. Though each player is comfortable with a toss that accommodates his or her individual style, there are common elements. Keep in mind that you want to contact the ball as high and as far in front of you as can be controlled. This ensures a flat trajectory and the desired velocity. The tossing hand keeps contact with the ball through the lift as long as possible. This allows you to be more accurate and to keep the ball from spinning. Toss the ball so that the horizontal panels are in front of the hitting hand. The ball is tossed from 8 to 18 inches above the vertically extended shelf hand (the hand that tosses the ball).

Contact is made with the meaty part of the hand, which is held straight and stiff throughout the motion. It must be emphasized that the point of contact be consistent and as high and as far in front of the head as you can control. As the server tosses the ball, the contact arm is pulled back (like pulling a bow string) with the stiff wrist and hand going up (Figure 4.9). The forward motion of this arm is coordinated with the weight transfer, accelerating it to the desired velocity at contact. You are trying to put a dent in the ball. It is important to try to go through the ball to the target to create the desired float. Some coaches will tell you to stop your hand on contact. If you accelerate your hand just prior to contact, it will appear that you are stopping, when, in actuality, the ball is slowing down the movement. Going through the ball ensures that you get an accurate trajectory and pinpoint the target. If you hit the side of the ball or break your wrist over or under the ball, it will spin and, therefore, be easier for the opponent to pass. Spin serves can be effective when maximum velocity is applied; however, every player should develop a float serve. It needs to be a staple on your menu.

A well-hit float serve is unpredictable. The server has a general idea of where it is going, yet the receiver must guess. Its velocity is hard to read because there is no spin. The trajectory is erratic because, without spin to cut through the various atmospheric conditions, the ball is at the mercy of velocity, air currents, humidity, and the laws governing the reparation of the dent put into the inflated ball by the contact hand. The good float serve will dip, bob, weave, rise, and perform other gyrations, making it difficult to receive. You know that your serve is respected if you hear wily veterans refer to it as a "heat seeker" or a "dark serve."

OTHER SERVES

As previously written, all serve variations are executed with the same basic elements and principles. The overhead, or "bow-and-arrow," float serve is the most common. An alternative is the roundhouse float serve (Figure 4.10). Its only

Figure 4.10   Roundhouse float serve

advantage is that some people find it to be an easier skill mechanically, using fewer arm movements. A brief description of other serves and their technical considerations and tactical application follows.

Underhand Float Serve

This serve is used most commonly by inexperienced players. Many players gaining newfound levels of volleyball skills have a tendency to look down their noses at the underhand serve. Yes, it carries a wimpy reputation, but it can be very accurate, can be floated every time, and is simple to execute. Even for "good" players, it is not a disgrace to hit the underhand float—especially if it yields results (Figure 4.11).

Figure 4.11   Underhand float serve

Standing Spike Serve

If the float serve is to volleyball what the knuckleball is to baseball, then the spike, or spin, serve represents the fast ball. Smoke. The heater. It relies on overpowering velocity and is intimidating. The standing spike serve is the simplest of the spins. The object is to get the ball to the receiver as fast as possible without giving him or her time to adjust. Toss the ball with two hands above and in front of your head. Use a spiking motion to contact the ball as high and as hard as you can control. The hand snaps over the top of the ball, creating maximum topspin so that the ball drops dramatically at the termination of its flight (hopefully over the net and inside the opponent's court—Figure 4.12).

Jump Spin Serve

This is the most dynamic, dramatic serve. It requires an accelerating approach, coordinated with either a one- or two-handed toss, a jump, and a spike. The objective is to contact the ball as high and as far in front of you *and* as close to the net as possible, requiring the toss to be located inside the court to accommodate a broad jump that uses the back line as a long jump toe board. The consequences are the same if you violate a long jump toe board or the volleyball back line: It is a foul. The jump spin maximizes force, velocity, and intimidation. It requires consistent control of several components that must be efficiently orchestrated: the toss (much higher than the bow-and-arrow toss), the approach (two or three steps), the jump (the arms swing upward as in spiking), and arm swing to contact (exactly like spiking) (Figure 4.13). It is fun and sure to impress anyone.

a.   b.

Figure 4.12   Standing spike serve

a.   b.

Figure 4.13   Jump spin serve

Sidewinder Serve

This is a variation of the standing spike and jump spin serves. When contacting a spike serve, your hand breaks at the wrist over the top of the ball. When hitting a sidewinder serve, your hand breaks around the side of the ball that is opposite its intended direction. The sidewinder serve is effective when mixed in with straight spins and floats. It is like a curveball in baseball.

Sky Ball Serve

This serve can only be used where there is enough vertical height to elicit the image of the serve's name. If the ball is not hit high enough, then it becomes a pitiful, easily passed ball known as "cotton candy" or, simply, "candy" (as in taking candy from a baby). The key to the effectiveness of the sky ball is the height it attains. To the receiver it should look like an aspirin tablet plummeting from the heavens and feel like a bowling ball when it hits the arms. Outdoors, the ball is at the mercy of the wind, and the receiver must contend with the sun or a white background of sky on a cloudy day. Indoors, it can only be used in big arenas. The main problem with the sky ball is accuracy. It can be somewhat embarrassing if at a critical moment in a game you launch one into the ocean or the third deck. This serve uses either an exaggerated underhand float technique or a modified side-arm technique, contacting the underside of the ball. Whatever technique you use, remember to consider the environmental conditions.

TACTICS

The serving ready position is the only time during play when you can take matters in your own hands and have exclusive control over what is about to happen. When you practice serving, it is critical to repeat the mental process in the ready position. Take a deep breath. Relax. Review the game situation. Review the game plan. Review the targets. Adjust your starting position, face the selected target, and eyeball your opponent. Let him or her know you are going to launch in his or her direction. Mentally isolate the target. Remember, you are in control and want to apply as much pressure with your serve as possible. Look over the opponent. Exude confidence. Appear to be perusing the selection of targets before you finally settle on one. Adjust your starting position a couple of times, appearing to get the right distance and angle to the mark. Eyeball the target. You have five seconds to perform this drama. It is plenty of time. Every time you serve, think, This is what I am going to do. If you concentrate on, "just getting it in," you probably won't. All players at one time or another worry about what their teammates will think if they miss. No one likes to see the rolling eyeballs and hear the unflattering words muttered under the breath by teammates. When learning the serve, practice the mental preparation every time in the ready position and the above concerns will not be factors.

LEARNING AND PRACTICING SERVING

It is almost time to quit reading about serving and go out and do it. Whichever serve you are going to try, remember these points:

1. In the ready position, mentally review where you are going to serve and why.
2. Face your target.
3. Toss the ball consistently each time.
4. Contact the ball as high and as far in front of your head as can be controlled (except for a sky ball serve).
5. Be compact. Avoid flailing your arms and legs.

Remember these learning keys:

1. Toss
2. Step
3. Hit

It is important to note here that in the bow-and-arrow serve, the toss and step are almost simultaneous, so it would read: "toss/step." If you were to verbalize the rhythm of the serve it would be "Ooomm . . . PAH! (Toss/step . . . HIT!)

Practice Activities

> *Boy! aahh, ah say BOY! Ah see a lot of choppin' but no chips flyin'.*
>
> –Foghorn Leghorn

In practicing any skill, keep in mind a few key points. Perform it in a realistic, gamelike environment. Rote repetitions will attend to the static mechanics required to perform the skill but won't elevate your level of play unless you practice the skill in a gamelike environment. Certainly, get comfortable with the physical rudiments. But as soon as possible, practice gamelike activities. Listed below are some good serving activities to learn. Try to work with at least one other person.

Mechanics

Serving against a Wall

Put a length of tape at 2.24 meters (women's net height) or 2.43 meters (men's net height) on a solid, unobstructed wall. Be sure that the wall you choose can be used to hit balls against without irritating someone. If space permits, the tape should be 9 meters long—the width of a legal court—otherwise, adjust the length according to the space available. Mark a line on the floor surface 9 meters back from the wall. This line is 3 meters long and aligned with the right side of the wall tape, which represents the net. This duplicates the serving area on a volleyball court and the distance the back line is from the net (see Figure 2.1).

OBJECTIVE: This activity repeats the mechanics of the serve at the distance and heights required on the court.

ACTION: If possible, have a partner watch your technique and give you feedback. Also, it is ideal to videotape yourself. Review each step of the serve and try to serve as close to the top of the tape as possible without hitting it. If the distance seems too great and forces you to compromise, correct your technique, then move as close to the wall as needed for proper execution and serve over the tape. As soon as you are comfortable at one distance, move back until you are behind the line. Eventually serve from any distance beyond the back line as long as you are between the ends of the 3-meter serving line. As you become more comfortable, put X's on the wall above the tape. Try to hit them, score your hits, and make up games with yourself or partners.

ADVANTAGES: Only one ball is needed for many repetitions. You can use any space available. It is a great way to repeat mechanics and get feedback. Setup is easy. Shagging balls isn't necessary.

DISADVANTAGES: This activity isn't gamelike. It offers no pressure (unless the wall has windows). It doesn't allow you to practice mental preparation aspects.

Partner Serving

Serve back and forth over the net with a partner. A ball, a partner, and a net are needed. Set up the court as legally as possible. If you don't have a net, poles, or a court, use a rope and tie it between two objects. Make sure it is at the correct height and that there is enough court space.

OBJECTIVE: This activity perfects the ability to serve over a net and put the ball into the opponent's court.

ACTION: Get as far back from the net as possible without having to compromise technique to get the ball over. As soon as you are comfortable at any given distance, move back. Once you are comfortable at any legal distance, focus on accuracy. Have your partner move to different positions on the court and work on serving to that position (Figure 4.14). Trade off occasionally. Compete if the spirit moves you by devising some goal; for example, the fewest misses out of ten at any given distance wins. Then modify it with accuracy by having to get within a meter of your partner's position to score.

ADVANTAGES: This activity develops court sense. The physical environment is consistent with the game environment. It needs little setup, requires just one ball, and can have many opportunities to respond in a relatively short time.

DISADVANTAGES: It provides no real gamelike pressure. It requires a legal net setup or equivalent. No other related skills are involved, so serving is executed in a rote fashion and not at random, as occurs in a real game.

Serving Games

Horse

This activity requires a volleyball court, a ball, and a marking system for targets. Two or more players can play.

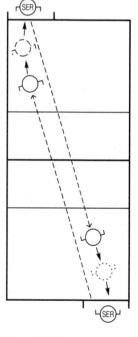

Figure 4.14
Partner serving

OBJECTIVE: This activity provides an opportunity to focus on accuracy and the related mental process.

ACTION: Like the traditional basketball game of "HORSE," the volleyball version requires one player to call his or her target before serving, the type of serve to be used, and from where he or she will serve. It is ideal to have taped areas on the opponent's court for accurate measurement of success of the called serve. If the first player accurately predicts his or her serve, then the second player must duplicate the type of serve, starting point, and hit the called target. If the second player successfully duplicates the first player's serve, the score remains the same. However, if the second player misses, then he or she picks up a letter. (If it's the first letter then it is an *H,* the second letter an *O,* and so on.) If a player misses his or her called serve, then the next player gets a chance to call a serve for his or her opponent to try to duplicate. The game continues until a player spells "HORSE." On the last letter (*E*), the player facing elimination has two chances to duplicate the serve or can opt to take one attempt and, if unsuccessful, require the other player to repeat the serve. If that player cannot successfully repeat, then the game continues. If he or she is accurate on the repeat, then the game is over.

ADVANTAGES: This activity forces concentration on the serve mechanics and accuracy in targeting. It pressures players to be accurate. It needs little setup and is fun.

DISADVANTAGES: It is not exactly gamelike because it only focuses on serving and not the real consequences of a good or bad serve.

Progressive Target Practice

This activity requires at least one court, although two or three courts next to each other is preferable to reduce congestion. The number of players who can participate is unlimited, within reason, and each player needs at least one ball. The drill can be timed, with the winner being the player who goes the furthest in the progression or the first player who completes all the targets.

Tape target areas down on the other side of the net, as shown in Figure 4.15. Each player needs at least one ball.

OBJECTIVE: This activity focuses on accuracy under pressure and practices mental preparation.

ACTION: The complete task is measured by how many courts and targets are available and marked. The number of times a target must be hit to progress is arbitrary. Each player must serve into a target before attempting the next target. Targets are listed in a sequential, predetermined order. The first player to complete the target list and related goal wins. An additional scoring system can include keeping track of the number of attempts to complete the course including the time it takes. This can be a game itself.

ADVANTAGES: This activity teaches the player to relax under the stress of time and numbers. It forces concentration. (You could also make a rule that states that if a player misses a serve, he or she must go back to the previous target or must add a successful serve to the present target.)

DISADVANTAGES: Progressive target practice uses block learning and not random learning, as is the case with the previous serving games.

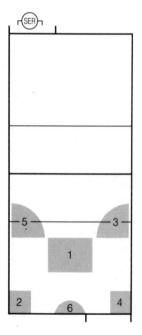

Figure 4.15

Progressive target practice

Sixty Serves

This activity requires the use of a court and at least one ball (many more are preferable for greater efficiency). Two teams of six players can be involved, but the game can also be adapted to fewer players.

ACTION: Each player gets 10 serves. Example: Player 1 on team A serves to team B. There is a rally with a natural conclusion. The team that wins the rally wins the point. Player 1 on team A continues to serve until 10 serves are completed. If the server misses a serve, it is a point for the receiving team. When player 1 on team A is finished, then player 1 on team B serves 10 times, both teams rotate, and the game continues until every player has served 10 balls. The final score simply reflects how many rallies a team wins out of 120 serves. Scoring can be modified by giving 2 points for an ace or taking points away for a miss.

ADVANTAGES: The focus is on serving in a gamelike situation. The consequences of the serve are obvious. It is random learning because the play continues after the serve, but it allows a player to go back and serve again, regardless of the previous play's outcome. The server can review the game situation, optimal target selection, and train the thinking process. Another, somewhat abstract advantage is the peer pressure this game creates. The server faces the scrutiny of teammates, because all are affected by the failure or success of the serve.

DISADVANTAGES: It is difficult to find enough players.

The above games and activities are but a few examples. There are no rule books, and they are certainly not cast in stone. Create your own games and activities. (For example, instead of taping down targets, use inflatable "Bozo" type punching clowns or an equivalent standing object.) The most important thing is to become a good server. Keep in mind the thought process of developing a learning activity:

- Become comfortable with correct mechanics. Remember the keys.
- Use gamelike activities as much as possible.
- Random learning is superior to block learning for long-term retention.
- Have fun.

To test your comprehension of the key elements of serving, turn to Worksheet 1 at the end of the book.

TROUBLESHOOTING
Serve

Problem	*Solution*
Attempted float serve spins.	Keep your toss consistent; keep your wrist locked; hit *through* the middle of the ball with the meaty part of the hand; accelerate your hand prior to contact (like throwing darts).

Problem

Ball goes long.

Solution

Move back; calm your adrenalin surge; focus on what you are going to do; keep the toss consistent and in front of and above your head; contact the ball as high and as far in front of you as can be controlled.

Problem

Ball goes short.

Solution

Move up; contact the ball higher relative to your head; time the weight transfer from your back to front foot as the hitting hand contacts the ball (the effect is that the body weight will transfer through the ball toward the target); accelerate the hitting arm/hand through the ball.

Problem

Trajectory is too high.

Solution

Contact the ball as high and as far in front of your head as can be controlled; contact the *middle* of the ball and follow through in line to the target.

Problem

Serve is inaccurate.

Solution

Keep hitting arm/hand in a direct line between the trailing leg and the target; point the lead foot to the target; be sure the toss is consistent every time and each serve is the same; be compact.

Forearm Pass

5

Forearm passing is the skill of contacting an incoming ball on the forearms and redirecting it to a predetermined target. It is commonly called *bumping*. Forearm passing is an *intermediate* contact skill. In other words, it is used to position the ball so that it can be set (when a player puts the ball in the air for a teammate to hit at the opponent) and/or attacked (when a player hits the ball directly at the opponent). It is the primary skill used in the serve receive. A modified forearm pass technique called the *J* (see Chapter 9) stroke is used for defensive retrieval so that a counterattack can be launched. The forearm pass is used to pass free and down balls. On occasion, when overhead passing cannot be used, forearm passing is the skill employed to set. Forearm passing is the most common skill in volleyball.

In terms of form and posture, it is very simple. When the incoming ball's velocity, trajectory, and final destination, coupled with the location of the target, require movement and positional adjustments, forearm passing becomes complex. It requires great concentration, reaction, and decision making. One of the opponent's tactical goals is to make your receiving tasks as difficult as possible. The opponent will try to drive you deep, smack it hard, drop it short, put it between you and a teammate, fake right and hit left, and otherwise tangle your feet as you attempt to reposition to pass with control. You can only counter the diabolical ploys of the opponent by mastering forearm passing and the related movements. You can do this by learning the mechanics and practice them through gamelike conditions as soon and as often as possible.

When first learning forearm passing, understand that your forearms are not used to taking a pounding. The related flesh will get red, sting, and sometimes bruise. Counter this by wearing a tight-fitting long-sleeve shirt. Make sure to practice with a high-quality leather volleyball. Synthetic leather and plastic balls will punish your forearms.

GAME APPLICATION

Since forearm passing is an intermediate skill, there is little direct tactical application. However, because it is the most widely used volleyball skill, accurate forearm passing is essential to the successful execution of team tactics. (At advanced levels of play, subtle changes in passing trajectory or setting direct to an attacker could be construed as specific tactics.)

MECHANICS

The serve receive is the most common example of the forearm pass, so it will be used in the following discussion unless otherwise indicated. The ready position is very similar to an athlete's ready position in other sports: a basketball defensive player, a football defensive back, a shortstop, a hockey player prepared to face off (without a stick). The feet are comfortably spread about shoulder width, with one foot slightly behind the other. The feet are pointed toward the impending action, with the weight mostly on the balls of the feet. The knees are flexed comfortably, slightly inside and in front of the big toes. The body is flexed comfortably at the waist, with the back straight and leaning forward so that the chin is slightly in front of the knees. The head is up, the eyes looking toward the source of the incoming ball. The arms and hands are held relaxed, either inside and slightly in front of the knees or placed lightly on the top of the corresponding thighs near the waist.

Notice the words "comfortably," "relaxed," and "lightly." Exact angles and percentages are not given because each person is built differently. The objective is to get ready to move and to make a controlled contact on the ball. The ready position is not necessarily a comfortable one, especially if held for a long time. The key is to assume it when necessary. The more you play, the more efficient you will become in assuming appropriate postures at appropriate times. It is very important to be *intense* but not tense, *relaxed* but not slumbering, and *balanced forward,* ready to move with controlled quickness and efficiency (Figure 5.1).

Aldis Berzins (U.S. Men's Volleyball Team 1978–1986, Olympic, World Cup, and World Championship gold-medal-winner) and Karch Kiraly (U.S. Men's Volleyball Team 1981–1989, World Cup, World Champion, and two-time Olympic gold-medal-winner) are considered the two best serve receivers the world has ever known. It is interesting to watch them prepare to receive serve, whether it is in a practice or in the final moments of a world-title match. They almost look disinterested prior to the serve. But they are mentally preparing for the upcoming play. Then, as the server begins final preparations and the referee's whistle blows, Aldis and Karch get ready in rhythm with the server's ministrations, assuming a ready position, opening their eyes as wide as possible, and focusing on the origination of the serve. They repeat the same preparatory movements every time. They never waste energy by assuming a ready position before it is required.

Figure 5.1
Forearm pass ready position

Movement and Footwork

At this point, it is necessary to cover movements related to all ball-handling situations. When serving, all movements are controlled by your design and whim. In passing situations, the ball's trajectory, velocity, ultimate destination, and your starting position dictate the required postures and movements. The more controlled your team is in handling the ball, coupled with the discipline of the offensive and defensive system employed, the simpler the movements needed. Are you impressed with the control a great pool player has when "running a table"? The shots look easy, the control obvious. You get stoked to try it. But when you begin your "run," the balls go all over the place. All the shots appear difficult. The experience snowballs: The more difficult the shot, the more you chase the elusive balls and contort your body to get a shot instead of "running the table." Volleyball is a big-ball pool game. The more control, the more compact the moves are to get into position to play the ball.

When getting into position to redirect the ball there are some basic principles:

1. Arrive at the point of contact *before the ball*.
2. Be in a position to be able to *play the ball in front of you, between you and your teammates* (Figure 5.2).
3. Be *stopped, balanced, and facing the ball* when making contact.

Sometimes the attainment of these principles is impossible. But if your movement skills are efficient and you work hard at getting in good contact position, the principles will have function. And, if your team is in harmony with this focused play ethic, "running the table" will be consistently possible.

Efficient footwork is essential to maintaining balance and establishing a stable contact position. Take advantage of *natural* movement tendencies when possible. If these natural tendencies prove ineffective, then prescribed patterns must be learned.

When there is time to prepare for an incoming ball that has a high trajectory or a ball that is within a couple of meters, the two-step *shuffle* is best. You always face the ball. Maintain a relative ready position throughout the shuffle (Figure 5.3). Use this as often as possible.

Lateral adjustments that either require covering a significant distance or an incoming ball's flat, fast trajectory demand a cross-step, or *turn-and-run* move. It is slightly more complex than the shuffle because you first must come out of the ready position and then reposition to make good contact (Figure 5.4).

Moving forward is the easiest adjustment, unless your weight is on your heels in the ready position. It seems prudent to sit back on your heels when faced with an opposing attacker, waist high over the net, ready to tee up on a perfect set, with no block between you and this slavering, seemingly merciless human weapon of destruction. Then, the opponent tips. The ball falls in front of you a step away, and you fall on your fanny. This action is guaranteed to elicit some furrowed brows and the appropriate verbal response.

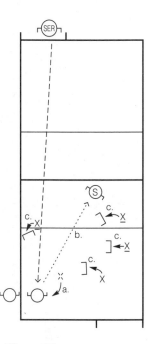

Figure 5.2

Getting into position: (a.) passer arrives at point of contact before ball; (b.) passer faces incoming ball and passes to target (S-setter); (c.) other players, while preparing for next responsibility, open up to passer in case of errant pass. (Underscored positions represent front-row players.)

Figure 5.3 Shuffle

Figure 5.4 Turn-and-run move

Maintaining a forward ready position under such circumstances is difficult but necessary. Moving forward is accomplished best with a *hop step*. Simply take the necessary steps to get to the point of contact and adjust into the contact position (Figure 5.5).

Moving backwards can be difficult but does not need to be. Keeping in mind that you want to always face the ball, *backslide* (Figure 5.6). Similar to the lateral shuffle, immediately determine which side of the body is going to lead the retreat. Similar to how an outfielder adjusts to a deep fly ball, get "off line" so you can adjust the rebound angle to pass to the target at the contact point. For example, if you were going to pass the ball on your right, then you would drop your right foot back and shuffle or "slide" back to the contact position. It is important to note

a.

b.

Figure 5.5 Hop step

Figure 5.6
Backslide

here that in serve receive situations where the ball is served down the line on the receiving team's left side, most accomplished passers prefer to drop the left foot back and dip the right shoulder toward the target area. The left-side receiver plays somewhat inside the court. A serve can come down the line to the outside of the receiver and not allow for the ideal contact position. Therefore, the conditions dictate the move.

On occasion, you will have to cover great distances to pursue a playable ball—any ball that has air between it and the floor or other immovable object. You must turn and run to the point of contact before the ball gets there. The final retrieval technique used is solely dependent upon when you arrive relative to the ball.

Whatever move is required to get to a good, controlled contact position, develop the ability to stop and face the ball and target. To do this, a *brake step* is required. It is intentionally spelled the same as an essential component in your vehicle because it has the same function: stopping. In control, facing your target with the ball in between. In volleyball, this is accomplished by planting the foot nearest the target and turning so that the toes are pointing in the direction of the intended pass (Figure 5.7). Sometimes this cannot be accomplished because the move would cause a dislocated ankle and knee. But make your best effort to follow through to the target. Once the inside foot is established, then the rest of the body will swing around and redistribute the weight.

There are many good players who plant the outside foot and are successful. However, this usually leads to momentum carrying the body away from the target and thus requiring a compensating movement with the contact surface (forearms or hands).

The basic principles concerning arriving at the point of contact before the ball—balance, stability, facing the ball, and contacting the ball through to the target—are consistent in every volleyball skill. As you practice and experiment with the related movements, keep these principles in mind.

Figure 5.7 Brake step

a.   b.

Movement Keys

When playing in drills or games, remember these movement-related keys:

1. *Read* the situation as it unfolds.
2. *Anticipate* what is going to happen.
3. *React* to the actual occurrence.
4. *Adjust* to the point of contact before the ball arrives.
5. *Retrieve* with control.

These movement-related keys form the important acronym RARAR.

Contact

Just prior to ball contact on the forearms, the body is in the ready position previously described and modified to accommodate the trajectory and speed of the incoming ball. Get low enough so that you can play the ball on your extended forearms.

Figure 5.8
Forearm contact surface

The forearm contact surface is created by putting the wrists and thumbs together, with the back of one hand crossing the palm and fingers of the other (Figure 5.8). The thumbs are pointed down to create an even, symmetrical rebound "platform." The shoulders are extended toward the hands to allow you to play the ball in front of your waist, as far away from your body as can be controlled (Figure 5.9). If you tried to play the ball close to your body, you could not manipulate the angle of deflection. You would get jammed. Contacting the ball away from the body allows you to adjust the contact platform and ensure the redirection of the ball to the intended target.

Figure 5.9
Forward contact ready position

There are other methods of locking the hands together to ensure a symmetrical forearm platform. Two or more fingers can be interlaced between the first and second knuckles of each finger. The fist of one hand can be tucked into the palm of the other. Many great beach players never connect the hands but simply put the wrists together. The hand position described above and illustrated in Figure 5.8 is the most versatile and accommodates all of the functions of forearm passing.

Modifying the Rebound Angle   Volleyball is a game of angles. Rarely is a ball played back toward the point of origination. Most of the time the ball is deflected at an angle from its incoming path to its outgoing path. Hopefully this deflection is done with premeditated intent and control. It is a fact that if a ball hits you, it will bounce off and go somewhere. The contact should be controlled. The angle of your forearm platform at the moment of ball contact will determine the angle and trajectory of the outgoing rebound. It would be ideal if you could face the target at the moment of contact. But, since the objective of the opponent is to put you in compromising positions, seldom can your total posture be readjusted. Therefore, you need to *drop the shoulder* nearest the target. This naturally raises the other shoulder. This action modifies the forearm platform and will deflect the ball in the desired direction (Figure 5.10). Another important element of controlling this rebound angle is the forearm contact angle relative to the ball. If the forearms are under the ball, the trajectory will be high; if the forearms contact the back of the ball (the side nearest the body), the outgoing trajectory will be flat (Figure 5.11). Finally, there is the matter of controlling the velocity of the outgoing ball. Learn to assess the speed and angle of the incoming ball quickly. Then, calculate how much impetus or cushioning is required to get the ball to the target. This is coordinated with the related posture adjustments and necessary footwork. Good passers have "quiet arms." They use minimum movement and never flail.

Figure 5.10
Modifying the rebound angle—dropped shoulder

Point of Contact   This term is used repeatedly. The point of contact is where you and the ball finally meet during any given phase of the game. *It is important*

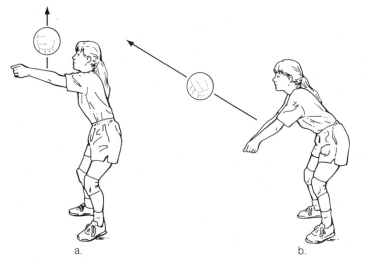

a.   b.

Figure 5.11   Modifying the rebound angle—forearm contact angle

that you control this crucial moment. This is why it is important that all skills are practiced in gamelike situations—so that specific, real-time movement can be repeated. *In order to control the point of contact you must be there first.* This is one of two overriding keys to winning volleyball: Arrive at the point of contact before the ball. The players and teams that can do this in all ball-handling situations will have the best control. (The second overriding key to winning volleyball can be found in Chapter 7.) In forearm passing, get your feet established before any other action takes place. Almost simultaneous with the feet, the body assumes the flexed, precontact position. Then, within a split second, the forearm rebound platform is readied. The ball arrives and is sent on its way to its intended destiny.

It is important to note that the ball should be played somewhere *between the knees and the waist* (Figure 5.12). It is preferable to play the ball *lower* than higher to the floor. The higher and closer to your body the ball is played, the less control you will have. Therefore, work hard every time at getting into good position when playing the ball.

Some players wonder what they should be looking at during this process. It is simple: Keep your eyes on the ball, but keep your head still. It is virtually impossible to visually track the ball to contact with your forearms. If you try, your head will bob and compromise a stable passing posture. Therefore, watch the ball in the bottom of your periphery while keeping your head stable.

Learning Keys

1. Arrive at the point of contact *before* the ball.

2. Face the incoming ball.

3. Place your wrists *together*.

4. Pass through the ball to the target.

You can't learn this finesse skill by reading about it. It is time to get up and get after it.

Figure 5.12
Contact between knees and waist

Practice Activities

Skill throws more weight than strength.

　　　　　－Cowboy saying

Forearm passing is an integral part of virtually every phase of volleyball. There-fore, you can practice the skill all the time. Presented here are some basic activities that require little equipment but are high on creativity.

Triads

Three players and two balls are needed. One player is a target; the second, a tosser; and the third, a passer—the player performing the primary ball handling. It is preferable, but not required, that a volleyball court and net be set up.

　　ACTION: The *tosser* (TO in Figure 5.13) has one ball and is near the net facing the *passer* (P) in the backcourt. The *target* (T) has the other ball and is to the left of the tosser near the net (where you want the ball passed). The basic drill has the tosser using a two-hand underhand toss to the passer, making him or her move to reposition to pass the ball. As soon as the tosser has let fly, the target *bounces* the next ball to the tosser so that it rebounds up to the tosser's hip. This is an important phase as it allows for the tosser to keep a rhythm to the drill. The passer passes the tossed ball to the target. As soon as the ball is passed, the tosser launches the next ball and the target bounces the other ball to the tosser. Triads can be measured by time. For example, each segment lasts 2 minutes. After the time expires, the players rotate and continue. It also can be measured by the number of perfect passes against total attempts. Create your own measuring systems to make it interesting, fun, and gamelike.

　　ADVANTAGES: By changing distances, target positions, and methods of pro-pelling the ball from the tosser, the triad drill can accommodate virtually every ball-handling situation. For example, the tosser can become a *server*. Either going to the opponent's serving area or somewhere in between, he or she can serve instead of toss. The tosser can become a *hitter,* standing on a box on the opponent's side of the net and spiking the ball at the passer. The target and passer can be positioned anywhere on the court to duplicate any situation. Use of space is also an advantage. Two groups of three can work on one side of the net. If you have more than three players, rotate in at one or more of the positions. (This reduces time with the ball but may be needed organizationally.)

　　DISADVANTAGES: It is difficult if there is just one ball or fewer than three players.

The Roof

Just you and one ball? No one around to play with? No court? Try the roof. Loosely adapted from a tennis drill in which a player volleys the ball against a chain link fence and must respond to the unpredictable ricochet, this drill requires a slanted roof (preferably with cedar shakes) for greater ricochet potential, you, and a ball.

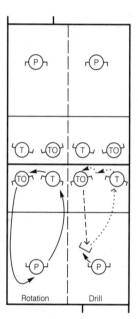

Figure 5.13
Triads

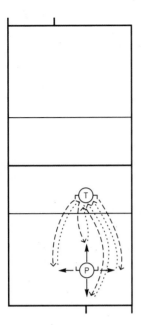

Figure 5.14

Points of the compass

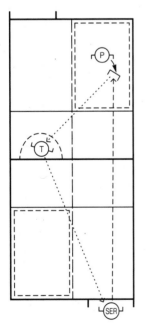

Figure 5.15

Three-point serve-receive game

ACTION: Simply toss the ball up on the roof and let nature take its course. The ball will gain momentum, plummeting back down the slant, careening off the shingles or vent pipes, finally boinging off the gutter. You are in a ready position prepared for any required movement to get to the best precontact position possible. React and pass the ball to a predetermined target. (Make sure it is *not* a plate glass window or an award-winning garden.)

ADVANTAGES: You can *create* opportunities to practice as long as you have a ball. This activity is only one example. It is obviously not ideal but does address reactions, related movements, adjustment of good precontact postures, and passing. Create other drills to practice quality contacts. Gamelike conditions may be difficult to design, but any contacts (as long as correctly performed) are better than none.

DISADVANTAGES: This activity specifically can cause some familial or community problems. If you do not own the building the roof covers, then the occupants could be irritated with the racket or anticipated destruction of the playing and/or target areas.

Points of the Compass

This activity requires two players and one ball. One player is the tosser/target, and the other is the passer.

ACTION: The distance can vary between the players. It is governed by skill level and the restrictions of the playing area. The *tosser/target* (T in Figure 5.14) tosses or hits the ball within 1 to 2 meters of the *passer* (P) in any direction. The passer reacts and passes the ball back to the target/tosser. The tosses or hits can be in a predetermined order or random. They should be difficult enough to test the range of the passer but not impossible. If the ball is being hit, it can be struck directly off the pass from the receiving player. This is one type of a defensive drill called *pepper* (see Chapter 9). Measurement is by time or total number of successful repetitions.

ADVANTAGES: Simply executed, this activity does not require an elaborate setup.

DISADVANTAGES: It is not very gamelike and can get boring.

Three-Point Serve Receive Game

Similar to a triad drill, the three-point game requires three players, one or more balls, a court, and a net. It specifically works on serve receive but can be adapted to free- and down-ball situations. It also provides practice for the server. The "game" creates the lessons in this activity. The object for the server and passer is to score three points in a row. The third player is the target, standing in the area where the ball is to be passed. The target player is also the judge on who scores the points.

ACTION: The server (SER in Figure 5.15) serves into the preset receiving area. This area is arbitrary, based on the focus of the drill and range of both the server and receiver. The server tries to hit his or her most effective serve. The receiver (P) tries to accurately pass the ball to the target (T). The target determines the accuracy and playability of the pass. He or she either awards the receiver or server the point based on his or her judgment. If the target player can reach the ball with one step without moving the "pivot" foot as used in basketball and determines that the height and velocity allow for easy access to playing the ball, then the point is awarded to the receiver. If the pass is not acceptable, the point goes to the server. A serving error is a point for the receiver. The first player to score three points in a row wins the game. Except for the beginning of each game, one player always has at least one point. For example, if the server has two points and serves into the net, the receiver then has one point and the server has none. When a game is completed, the target player and the winner exchange places and a new game begins.

ADVANTAGES: The game situation focuses on the inherent pressure of the serve-receive confrontation with measurable results. Tournaments can be played with this activity. It also is a good serving drill.

DISADVANTAGES: The target player can wait a long time between action. This can be alleviated by having the target player set each pass.

Other games and activities described in other chapters will require forearm passing and provide many opportunities for quality contacts. Games such as doubles and triples are live-fire passing activities in which the control or the lack of control will have obvious, consequential results.

To test your comprehension of the key elements of forearm passing, turn to Worksheet 2 at the end of the book.

TROUBLESHOOTING
Forearm Pass

Problem	*Solution*
Ball goes back over net.	Keep arms still; make contact on the *forearms* if the ball is hitting on the hands; make forearm contact on the *bottom* of ball so that it goes up; arrive before the ball; be *stopped* when passing.
Problem	*Solution*
Passes are too low.	Contact the ball on the forearms *as far away from your body* as can be controlled; make contact *under* the ball.
Problem	*Solution*
Ball jams passer.	Keep hips *away* from the contact point; *use a backslide* to adjust your floor position.
Problem	*Solution*
Ball goes behind during pass attempt.	Bend your knees so that ball contact is made between the waist and knees; keep the ball away from the body; see solution for jams.

Overhead Pass

6

Overhead passing describes the location of the ball relative to the body when contact is made, unlike forearm passing, which describes where on the body the ball is contacted. Overhead passing is the skill most often used in setting the ball for an attacker to hit. It is also used in passing situations where the trajectory of the incoming ball allows for overhead passing. It is the ball-handling skill of choice if possible. Ultimately, the use of overhead passing in ball-control situations allows for faster transition play. It is also more accurate than forearm passing.

However, almost all beginners opt for forearm passing in every ball-control play because it is initially easier and has a feeling of better control. But, alas, it is not so. Forearm passing is best for controlling flat trajectories and fast-traveling balls. It is also superior for the retrieval of balls that dribble over the net and require a low-postured, scooping maneuver. And it is used to run down deflected balls that must be redirected over long distances. But overhead passing is superior when the incoming ball is slow and high. It is used for precision control. If forearm passing were likened to a meat cleaver in the hands of a butcher cutting up a side of beef, then overhead passing would be the scalpel in the hands of a surgeon performing delicate surgery. All players must master overhead passing, but it is the setter who must be exceptionally adept at this skill.

GAME APPLICATION

Similar to forearm passing, overhead passing is an *intermediate* skill. It is most often used in support of the team attack strategies. Occasionally, it is used to place the ball on the opponent's side of the net in third-contact situations. This is known, politely, as an *attack volley* but is considered a wimpy effort. The setter's application of overhead passing, known as *setting,* is considered the most tactical part of volleyball. Choices of who and where to set, the height and speed of the set, and what is best in each situation, makes a setter a true surgeon.

MECHANICS

The ready position is the same as that used in forearm passing. The reason for this is simple: You don't know which skill to use until you gauge the trajectory and velocity of the ball and calculate the distance the ball needs to travel to get to the point of contact. Because overhead passing requires a more specific posture than forearm passing, try to overhead pass all free balls and sets to force you to concentrate on always getting into good position.

The basic rules governing ball handling legislate that 1. during play, no ball can come to a visible rest on any legal contact surface; 2. no ball can contact two different body parts on the same attempt to play the ball unless it is the first contact after the opponent has sent it over the net; 3. the ball can only be played on any surface of the body on or above the knees. (In some volleyball circles, the overhead pass is known as the *face pass,* describing a legal but not preferable contact surface. The face pass is not used in this book.) The specific rules describing legal contacts can be found in the USVBA's Annual Volleyball Guide and Rule Book, rule 8, articles 3–7. It is important to note that volleyball tradition demonstrates that officials are much more likely to ticket an overhead pass than a forearm pass. Never, *never* glance over at an official if you think your overhead pass wasn't clean. The newer you are to the game, the more likely an official will scrutinize your overhead technique. This is true at any level. It is why many players avoid using the overhead technique. It is also why you must work hard to get into good contact position so that it looks like you are in control.

Three Posture Ranges

Volleyball is played in three postures relative to the floor. The *low range* requires postures that accommodate a ball played near the floor. These include digging, collapses, dives, rolls, and sprawls (see Chapter 9). Although most of these techniques use either forearm passing or one-hand/arm contact, the collapse and digging position can be used to overhead pass.

The *middle range* requires postures to play the ball between the knee and slightly above the head while the feet are on the floor. These include serving, serve receive, free- and down-ball passing, and setting. Overhead passing is used in all middle-range activity except serving and serve receive. It must be noted that forearm passing is used almost exclusively in serve receive and down-ball passing. It also can be discretely employed in free-ball passing and setting.

The *high range* requires postures to play the ball when jumping is involved. These techniques include most varieties of attack, jump serves, blocking, and jump setting.

It is important to note that overhead passing is the only volleyball skill intentionally used in all three posture ranges.

Footwork

The basic footwork is the same as establishing the ready position for forearm passing. However, more attention must be given to *facing the target* when passing the ball. It is difficult to control the ball directing it over a shoulder. The best way to get into the preferred position is to arrive at the point of contact before the ball, face the target, and get your hands up early. Review the general ball-handling footwork described in Chapter 5. Footwork for specific applications such as the collapse set and setter's responsibilities will be covered in the relative sections. During a front overhead pass, the weight is transferred from the back foot to the front through the ball.

Basic Posture

The basic posture of overhead passing can be described as a flexed position: feet approximately shoulder width apart with one foot comfortably ahead of the other; the body slightly bent forward at the waist with the back straight; the elbows comfortably spread and above the shoulders; the *hands ball shaped* and held approximately 3 to 6 inches above the hairline (if the hairline is receding, use the reference point where the forehead turns into the top of the head), the wrists cocked, thumbs pointed toward the eyes, fingers spread but relaxed; and the eyes looking through the hands at the incoming ball (Figure 6.1).

Figure 6.1
Basic overhead passing posture

Contact

Describing in words the contact of the fingers on the ball in overhead passing is difficult at best. It is something you must feel. In fact, this contact is commonly called *touch,* as in, "That setter has a great touch," or, "He has the touch of a nose tackle." Some players have a natural, soft touch. Other, accomplished players have great control but seem to have dowels for fingers.

The contact of the ball on the fingers can be likened to a diver on a diving board. The incoming ball primarily contacts the thumbs, forefingers, and middle fingers. The ring and little fingers touch the ball but act in a supporting role (Figure 6.2). The ball's inertia pushes down toward your head while the wrists move through the intended trajectory. Just as the diver begins his or her upward rebound when the board reaches its maximum flexed position, so the ball starts its outward and upward journey when the fingers are at maximum flexion. The palms are actually at the sides of the ball, and the thumbs, forefingers, and middle fingers are mostly under and behind it. The hands follow through the ball in the intended trajectory line. When learning the contact sequence, it is a good technique to extend your arms and hands until they make contact at the base of the thumbs. Then bring the hands back to the head reference point in a praying motion. This will ensure that you are putting symmetrical force and control through the ball

Figure 6.2
Contact

toward the target. When seen at speed, the various components of overhead passing are virtually impossible to distinguish. It appears that the ball nestles in the ball-shaped hands and silently springs out. The ball should not be spinning, and the contact should not be heard without a concentrated effort.

Basic Overhead Passing Sequence (Figure 6.3)

1. Assume a general *ready position.*
2. Identify the point of contact and get there *before* the ball.
3. *Face the target* while bringing up your hands early. (This action is similar to a gunfighter drawing two guns to the top of his head.)
4. Fix your hands in a *ball-shaped form.*
5. Contact the ball and send it in a *premeditated trajectory.*
6. *Follow through* with your hands until the base of the thumbs touch, and then *withdraw* your hands to the hairline in a praying motion.

VARIETY OF USES

Free-Ball Passing

A *free ball* is any ball an opponent returns over the net easily. It is done to try to keep the ball in play rather than place it tactically. Usually it has a slow, high trajectory. A free ball is almost always sent over the net by a forearm pass or an overhead pass.

Figure 6.3   Basic overhead passing sequence

Most players receiving a free ball handle it on their forearms, regardless of the effort's complexity or simplicity. The principles governing any ball-control play are: 1. use the simplest technique; and 2. attempt tactically what you can control technically. A free ball translated in Japanese means a "chance ball." The meaning is the same: You get a free chance to run a counterattack. It is strongly recommended here to *overhead pass* every free ball. The tempo of the counterattack can be controlled with more accuracy. The turnaround time is quicker. The ball is contacted sooner than waiting to bump it. Try to get into the habit of overhead passing the free ball to ensure that you always get into good position at the point of contact and try to initiate play. The key is to know when to use which skill. This takes practice and playing experience.

Attack Volley

If you are on the side that must give up a free ball, refer to it as an *attack volley* to make it sound like every play has some strategical implication. If the ball must be set back to the opponent and it is not able to be spiked, you want to control its placement and trajectory. The best way to do this is to use the overhead passing technique. If you can jump and pass it, so much the better. However, if you can jump, you should be able to hammer the ball. Attack volley is a safe control play. When no other attack option is available, it is a wise selection. However, if it is used as a primary attack play, then it becomes a timid effort and will bring on teammate scowls like bears to honey. Further, you won't get many sets if the attack volley is the main weapon in your arsenal. Remember this principle: In any given situation, use the most effective skill that you can control.

Setting

Setting can be divided into three categories: 1. technique (the ability to control the set), 2. tactics (knowing who to set when and why), 3. leadership (the ability to get the best effort out of teammates). Setting is perhaps the most specialized of the *tactical* skills. Books are written on learning to set. It is a responsibility central to all team play. The setter is the hub of the wheel. The setter is like a quarterback, a point guard, a pitcher, a circus ringmaster, a film director, a . . . a . . . a. . . . You get the picture. The setter is in on every play. A hitter can rotate around and never touch a ball, whereas the setter makes contact on the second ball of each sequence of three. The setter has to make the right choice, deliver accurately, and be able to keep all fellow players happy in their roles. Though the setter must be a master of all ball-handling skills and related movements, the primary delivery system of the set is overhead passing. All players will set during the course of the game because of the ricocheting nature of volleyball. Basically, every player needs to be able to *front set* so that the ball will have a high trajectory. The ball should land 5 feet inside the court and 5 feet back from the net so that an attacking teammate can get a good approach and swing. The ball should appear to be coming off a waterfall.

The setter, however, must run an offense. To do this, he or she must be able to front set, back set, jump set, quick set, play set, and back-row set. He or she must also be able to mend the broken play, converting a marginal pass into a sweet, hittable set. All these techniques are tempered by the tactics. What hitters are available? Who is hot? How is the opponent's defense deployed? What is the game situation? What is the rotation?

The setter has *leadership* responsibility. All real volleyball players want to smack the ball. The setter determines who gets the chance. Keeping the peace among attack-ravenous teammates requires the ability to work with and lead people. Knowing when to pat someone on the butt or kick them in the butt is helpful. Even though a setter must have leadership ability and tactical knowledge, the emphasis here is on technique.

"Setting," as a *technical* term, is used more often than "overhead passing" because it is easier to say. (Let's go set a few balls, is less of a mouthful than, Let's go overhead pass a few balls.) However, it is very important to distinguish between the two even though they are connected because setting is tactically specific.

Specific Technical Setting Skills   The setter always tries to face the left side of the court because most offenses are designed with right-handed spikers and the most comfortable approach routes originate from the left side. (Approach routes are covered in Chapter 7.)

Collapse set   This is used when a ball is passed low and away from the net. The setter does everything possible to use an overhead pass. The key is getting the head under the ball. This is done by getting the foot nearest the net, usually the right, underneath the incoming ball's point of contact. As in the brake step described in Chapter 5, the foot is pointed toward the intended attacker. The posture is adjusted so that the ball can be handled overhead. The other foot swings around the brake, establishing as balanced a position as possible. The momentum of the move, coupled with the priority of getting a good contact on the ball, forces the player to sit down behind the heel of the leg furthest from the net. In the execution of this skill, both knees are pointed toward the target and neither should touch the floor (Figure 6.4).

One-foot pivot set   This set is similar to the collapse set, except it is used to handle a higher ball off the net and the setter stays on his or her feet.

Back set   In the back set, the setter directs the ball behind himself or herself to the hitter. A back set requires the same posture as the basic overhead pass.

Figure 6.4   Collapse set

However, instead of the weight being transferred from the back to the front foot, the opposite occurs. The back of the head should be in line with the intended trajectory. At the moment of contact, the back arches as needed and the head drops back toward the set. The player then follows through with the hands going back over the head in the trajectory line (Figure 6.5).

Jump set   In most complex offensive systems, the setter is required by coaches to jump set every well passed ball. This allows the setter to run a faster offense, especially to the quick hitters. It makes quicks and play sets easier to execute because the setter is closer to the hitters. The jump setter is a continual distraction to blockers, particularly when in the front row as a potential hitter on the second contact. The ball should be contacted as described in the basic overhead pass, but at the zenith of the setter's jump the hands must be up early so the setter can control the ball in ball-shaped hands and not jab at it (Figure 6.6). An important element of jump setting is knowing when to jump. Maximum control is the goal, and the setter must understand his or her range of abilities. This comes from practice and playing experience.

Setter Precontact Position   As a rule, volleyball players should establish a position so they can play the ball between themselves and the net. Setters however, need to get *between* the ball and the net (Figure 6.7). This allows them to set the

a.   b.   c.

Figure 6.5   Back set

Figure 6.6   Jump set

second ball between the attacker and the net and intercept any errant pass heading back to the opponent.

The setter needs to be at the target before the ball is contacted by the receiver. This is not always possible but should happen most of the time. The setter chases down a bad pass from the target and should never be en route while a teammate is passing serve.

The receiver should see the setter right of center, feet approximately shoulder width apart and at about a 45-degree angle to the net with a hand up. This allows the setter to see his or her teammates, the opponents over the right shoulder, and move to the point of contact if the ball is not in the target area.

The setter is the hub of the wheel and must establish a consistent target position every time. If he or she does not, then the setting will be erratic and will send a message to the passers, I don't expect a good pass, so I'll just wander around and see where you people might launch it.

Basic offensive tactics will be discussed in Chapter 12. The setter's role will be described. To master the art of setting, you must study and practice it. All of its components cannot be fully covered here.

Learning Keys

1. *Arrive* at the point of contact before the ball.

2. *Face* the target.

3. Get your *ball-shaped hands* up early.

4. *Follow through* and *pray back* high.

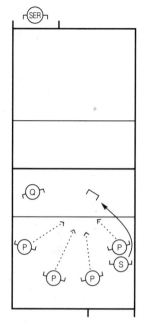

Figure 6.7

Setter precontact position in target area before the serve receive is contacted

Practice Activities

> *The best passing drills are* pass, *set, hit. The best setting drills are pass,* set, *hit. The best hitting drills are, pass, set,* hit.
>
> —Marv Dunphy, 1988 USA Olympic Gold Medal Coach

Why are you still reading this stuff? You can get familiar with the material by reading, but you learn it by *doing*. Sooo . . . let's roll.

The Setting Game

This game is fun. It also contradicts the principle of using gamelike activities. It is included because it is easy to organize and fun! You need a volleyball and a basketball half-court. It can be played by two or more players.

ACTION: Player A begins play by standing at the free throw line or top of the key. He or she tosses the ball to himself or herself and attempts to set the ball into the basket (Figure 6.8). If successful, player A scores the points awarded for that distance (see "scoring"). If the ball misses all of the apparatus, player B toes the

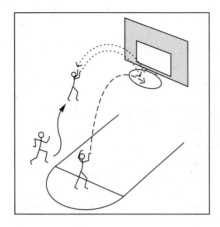

Figure 6.8 The setting game

mark and begins the action. However, if the ball does not go into the basket but bounces off the rim or backboard, it is ruled playable for player A to try to score. The ball must be played either directly off the rim or board or off one bounce on the floor. If the ball bounces more than once, play is concluded. The player who has scored last initiates play from either the free throw line or top of the key.

If more than two players are participating, they play the ball in sequence. For example, player A tosses and sets from the top of the key. The ball careens off the rim, bouncing on the floor to the right side of the key. Player B back sets the ball and it hits the top of the board. Player C is in position to set direct to the basket. However, player C gags, ricocheting the ball off the front rim. Player A is ready for the ball, taking it off the bounce on the floor and sets it into the basket for the score and the right to begin the next play from the free throw line or top of the key.

SCORING: The first player to score 21 points wins.

The Starting Play

overhead pass from the free throw line	1 pt
overhead pass from the top of the key	2 pts

Ensuing Play

front overhead pass off floor bounce	2 pts
front overhead pass off backboard/rim rebound	3 pts
back overhead pass off floor bounce	3 pts
back overhead pass off direct backboard/rim rebound	4 pts
front forearm pass off floor bounce	3 pts
front forearm pass off direct backboard/rim rebound	4 pts
back forearm pass off floor bounce	5 pts
back forearm pass off direct backboard/rim rebound	6 pts

ADVANTAGES: It is easy to find a place to play. This game is a great activity to practice ball-handling movements and contact positions. Players get to practice anticipation, reaction, correct contact postures, appropriate skill selection, and accuracy. Successful execution of these elements results in scoring.

DISADVANTAGES: It is not gamelike.

Ten-Foot Game

This game can be adapted to virtually all skills of volleyball. You need a net and a space approximately 30 feet wide by 10 feet deep. A full court with a 3-meter (10 foot) line is the easiest to use. Teams of one, two, or three players can play. One ball is required.

ACTION: The court is 9 meters (30 feet) wide and 3 meters (10 feet) deep. On a regular volleyball court, the game is played between the 3-meter lines (Figure 6.9). The teams play volleyball but must only use the overhead passing technique. It is a foul if a player is forced to use the forearms or other parts of the body to play the ball. There are three contacts allowable on each side. The serve can be either contacted with a toss-to-self overhead pass or regular serve technique. Regular or rally-point scoring can be used and played to any designated final point.

ADVANTAGES: This game is easily organized and adaptable to any space. It forces players to work hard to get into position to play the ball overhead and teaches the rudiments of tactical play. It has a control component because it requires receiving and delivering with accuracy in a relatively small space.

DISADVANTAGES: The applicable trajectories are generally low and are not often used in real volleyball. The restriction of using one skill only can force poor technique unless closely monitored.

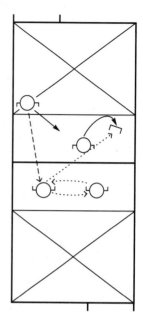

Figure 6.9
Ten-foot game

HORSE and "Around the World"

The traditional games of basketball of HORSE and "around the world" can be adapted to volleyball by simply changing balls. You need a volleyball and a basketball half-court. Use only overhead passing. Two or more players can play.

ACTION: The scoring of HORSE is described in Chapter 4. To play "around the world," players must first determine the setting marks on the itinerary around the world (usually the key area). Normally, each lane hash mark, the sides of the free throw line, and the top of the key are the stop-off points. A player begins at the first mark nearest the basket. He or she attempts to set the ball into the basket either directly or off the board. If the player is successful, then he or she moves to the next mark. The player continues to move sequentially from mark to mark until he or she misses (Figure 6.10). Except for the first play, the player has a choice to stay or set a second time. If the player makes it, he or she can move to the next mark and continue. If the second chance misses, the player returns to the beginning, loses his or her turn, and, after the other players complete their turns, starts again. The first player to successfully complete the journey wins.

ADVANTAGES: Both the HORSE and "around the world" drills have lots of contacts and focus on accuracy and relative trajectories under competitive stress.

DISADVANTAGES: The self-toss is not gamelike. No movement is required. Neither activity is gamelike.

Setter Chase

This can be a tough but effective drill. At least four players are needed, more are preferable, plus at least ten balls and a container.

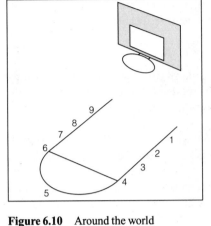

Figure 6.10 Around the world

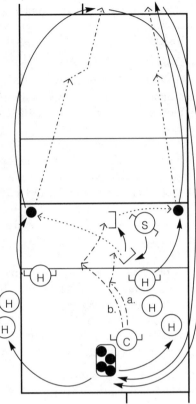

Figure 6.11 Setter chase

ACTION: Two or more spikers (H in Figure 6.11) are split between the outside hitting positions on the left and right sides of the court. The setter (S) begins at the target. A coach or another player (C) with the bucket of balls is approximately 2 meters in the court from the back line. That person either bounces or tosses a ball so that the setter must move to a good position to set to either spiking position. The setter always works to arrive at the point of contact before the ball, get stable and stopped, face the left-side hitting position, and set the ball overhead. As soon as a ball is set, another is immediately bounced or tossed, forcing the setter to relocate and set again. The spikers can either catch the ball or hit. If they hit, then each spiker must shag and return the ball to the bucket. It is optimal for the spikers to hit so that they also get practice. The drill can be measured by time, number of total repetitions, or judged acceptable sets.

ADVANTAGES: Gamelike movements are required. High intensity under fatiguing conditions makes the setter focus on every play in order to be accurate. The measurement of the drill determines the standard to which the setter must perform. The drill is adjustable, so spikers and blockers can be added.

DISADVANTAGES: Several balls, a container, a court, and at least four people are needed. The tosser/bouncer needs to be aware of the goals of the drill and know the physical limitations of the setter so that each repetition is challenging yet realistic.

Points of the Compass, Triads, and the Roof

These drills are applicable to overhead passing. Refer to the activity descriptions outlined in Chapter 5. Just use overhead passing instead of forearm passing. Of course, you can mix the skills. Most spiking drills incorporate both setting and passing skills.

To test your comprehension of the key elements of overhead passing, turn to Worksheet 3 at the end of the book.

TROUBLESHOOTING
Overhead Pass

Problem	*Solution*
Ball is inaccurate and does not go straight.	Arrive *before* the ball; face the target; be *stopped* when making contact; use ball-shaped hands; make contact above the hairline and follow through *symmetrically*.
Problem	*Solution*
Ball spins.	Arrive *before* the ball; get your hands up early; use ball-shaped hands; let the ball work on the fingers like a diver on a diving board; see the solution for inaccuracy, above.
Problem	*Solution*
Trajectory is too flat.	Arrive *before* the ball; be stopped; contact the ball *above* the hairline; keep your hips *under the fall line* of the ball; keep your hands *high* during the follow through.
Problem	*Solution*
Overhead pass has no power.	Arrive *before* the ball; contact the ball close to the head so that the elbow and wrist levers are completely available; *release quickly* without jabbing.
Problem	*Solution*
Back set falls short.	Contact the ball above the hairline; see solution for no power, above.

Attack

7

Attack skills include spiking (or hitting), tipping, roll (or half-speed) shots, and setter dumps, which will be described in this chapter. The attack is the entree on the volleyball menu. It is *the* terminal contact. Whoever puts the ball away receives accolades from teammates and fans alike. It is the skill that carries the most colorful verbs: kill, hammer, heat, smack, spank, crank, bury, smoke, rip, rap, pop, stick, stroke, sting, blast, beat, and crush it are but a few. Every real volleyball player wants to heat one up.

Just as "forearm passing," "bumping," and "serve receive" are synonymous among volleyball aficionados, so are "hitting" and "spiking" interchangeable with "attack." It is important to understand that attack embraces the individual skills as well as the team tactical skills.

Next to serving, spiking is the easiest skill to learn for most people. It can be frustrating for short players who have limited jumping ability because the object is to hit the ball down over the net. However, with practice, these athletes can be effective attackers at most levels of play.

GAME APPLICATION

Spiking is a terminal contact, so there are significant tactical options. The individual player needs to be able to hit a variety of shots and angles at different velocities. Coordinated routes and timing of several spikers make up the team attack. These tactical applications will be covered later in the chapter.

MECHANICS

Attack Principles

- A hitter must make himself or herself *available* so that the setter can set the ball between the hitter and the net.

- The hitter *accelerates* to the attack.
- The hitter must get a *good swing* at the ball.

The following keys are really extensions of the above principles:

The A Keys

- Available
- Approach
- Ascend (or get Air)
- Attack

Through the whole sequence you must *accelerate!*

Available

If you are going to be an effective attacker, you must *make yourself available.* Being unavailable is probably the most common ingredient in a down or free-ball return. The most crucial element in creating the opportunity to hammer the ball is to get into a starting position so that the setter can set between you and the net. You must create enough room to fully approach, jump, and swing. Beginning players who appear to have spiking mastered because they can hit a ball against a wall or hit a tossed ball over the net often never seem to get a good swing in a game. Typically, they will blame poor serve receive or erratic setting. Most often, the beginning spiker does not make himself or herself available by adjusting to the unfolding situation. You will notice that the great players always get a good swing. In serve receive situations, the spikers are usually in the optimal starting positions. If the serve receive is not accurate, then the spikers must adjust *so that the setter can set the ball between the spiker and the net* (Figure 7.1).

In the transition, or rally, making yourself available is more difficult. Often, you are at the net blocking and must get away from the net to the starting position. Furthermore, the accuracy of the pass in transition is less than in serve receive. You must always *track the ball* with your eyes. New players will often turn around at the net as if they were on a ledge. The ball is then set to them and they cannot get an approach and must either passively bump or set the ball over the net.

It cannot be emphasized too much: *Make yourself available!* Get away from the net. Get an approach. When practicing spiking, make sure to begin where you might be in a game—at the net, from serve receive, from chasing down an errant ball outside the court.

When you practice, don't get into the habit of standing in a spiking line, tossing the ball to a standing setter, and hitting an easy, perfect set. It never happens in a game.

Two Key Words   Success in volleyball can be reduced to two words: 1. *arrive* (the team whose players arrive at the point of contact before the ball will have consistent ball control) and 2. *available* (the team whose players are the most consistent in getting available to attack will score).

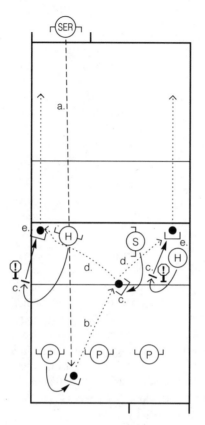

Figure 7.1

Available: (a.) server (SER) serves;
(b.) passer (P) passes; (c.) setter (S) goes
to point of contact and hitters (H) adjust
position to start approach so that setter can
set between hitter and net; (d.) setter sets;
(e.) hitters approach and hit.

Approach

The *run* is the approach. It is also a learning key for the approach because it
describes the action. The word "sprint" would be more like it, because *acceleration* is paramount to success. Actually, the final three steps are the most important.
For right-handers, left, right, left is the correct pattern. The steps leading up to
those final three are preparatory adjusting steps used during the available phase.
The left-right-left pattern used during the approach puts the hitter in an optimal
position for the jump and hit phases. The final, left step lands so that it is slightly
in front of the right and slightly turned toward the direction of the ball. This final
step acts as a brake step, converting horizontal movement into vertical deployment. The first left step is an accelerating one, lining up the hitter toward the
launch point. The second, or right, step is a long, quick movement that lands heel
first at the launch point. The final left step whips by the right, contacting the floor
almost simultaneously in the position described above. The rhythm of the final
three steps is leefftt . . . right/left! The sensation is one of acceleration (Figure
7.2).

Left-hand hitters approach right, left, right.

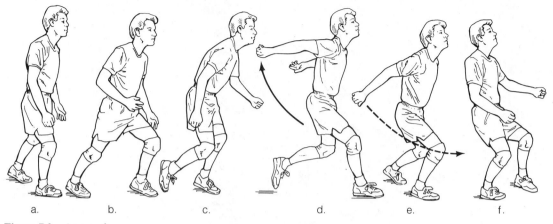

Figure 7.2 Approach

Ascend (or Jump)

A volleyball player's jumping ability is probably the most discussed and embellished physical trait. It is always interesting to hear how a retired player's "vertical" has increased during the post-playing years. Research tells us that jumping ability increases through training, yet it seems the telling of past glory is an easier, more effective way of improving one's jump.

Contrary to common myth, there is no such thing as "hang time." It's an illusion. You go up; you come down. The higher you jump, the longer you are in the air. You cannot hang around unless you are a marionette. Yet anyone can improve his or her jump. It can be done through resistance-strength-power training and improved jumping technique (including an accelerating approach). There are natural jumpers whose physiology gives them specific mechanical advantages. Likewise, there are those whose physical makeup is not conducive to great leaps. But remember: *Through training and practice, everyone can improve jumping ability.* It just doesn't seem fair that some can do so more easily than others. See player 5 in Figure 7.3. Notice how high he is relative to the net (at 8 feet) and player 9 (who is 6 feet 5 inches tall).

The jumping phase of spiking is the explosive transferal of horizontal acceleration to a vertical launch. The feet must be comfortably spaced about shoulder width apart to ensure a balanced takeoff. There will be a natural broad jump. It is important that it does not take away from a maximum vertical position. In some tactical situations, a broad jump is emphasized, such as in back-row, slide, and swing hitting.

As the second step of the final approach is being planted, both arms are extended as far back and as high as possible (Figure 7.4a). As the final foot lands, the legs are flexed relative to the player's strength, physiology, and control. The sharpest angle would be 90 degrees behind the knee. This radical angle requires great strength. The angle is much less for most players gathering position prior to launch. Explore the takeoff position that is most efficient for you.

Figure 7.3 The big jump

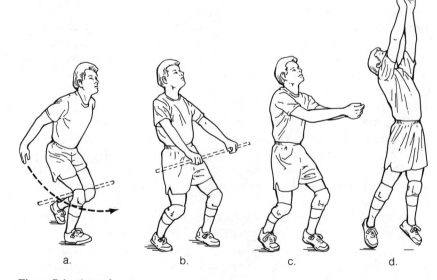

a. b. c. d.

Figure 7.4 Ascend

The horizontal movement is transferred skyward when the last step brakes and the arms are pulled through and up. It appears as if the player were grabbing a bar as his or her arms pass behind the flexed knees (Figure 7.4b). As the arms go vertical, the powerful quadriceps, hip flexors, gluteus maximus, and friends kick in and the body goes airborne (Figures 7.4c and 7.4d).

The words "powerful" and "explosive" should describe the feeling you have when jumping. To get better at jumping, *jump*. Do it a lot and do it right. Basic jump training and related resistance activities are discussed in Chapter 10.

Attack (or Hit)

Basically, spiking a volleyball is a throwing motion. Imagine the hitting arm as a whip, with the handle at the shoulder and the hand as its tip. A basic principle of hitting is: *Contact the ball as high and as far in front of your hitting shoulder as you can control* (Figure 7.5). You want to develop accelerating power coming from a shoulder rotation, or torque, through a whiplike action to the ball. In order to create this maximum, controlled force, keep the ball in front of you. It is important to contact the ball high in order to hit it over the net, manipulate the block, and have a variety of angles to attack.

Try to hit from behind the ball toward the intended direction with a relaxed, open hand and a loose wrist. This will give you plenty of force and maximum control. It is probably true that a ball could be hit harder with a closed fist clubbing the ball; however, the gain in velocity would be offset by a loss of control.

Figure 7.5 High and forward contact

The footwork in the approach allows for the natural shoulder rotation, or torque, to take place in the air. If you come in with opposite footwork, known as *goofy footing,* you would have to consciously twist to create shoulder rotation. This often leads to shoulder problems.

A Review of the Hitting Keys

1. Make yourself *available*. Get off the net. Adjust so that the setter can set the ball *between you and the net* and you can get a full approach.
2. *Approach* with an *accelerating,* 3-or-more-step *run*.
3. *Ascend* (jump). Convert horizontal acceleration to *vertical explosion*.
4. *Attack* (hit). The arm is a whip, with the shoulder as its handle and the hand as its tip. Contact with a *loose wrist* and *relaxed hand*.

INDIVIDUAL ATTACK TACTICS

Tipping

Tipping, or the exclusively American term "dinking," is volleyball's version of the change-up. The ball is contacted at the same point as described in hitting, requiring the same approach and jump. However, at the moment of ball contact, the wrist, hand, and fingers are *stiff.* Optimal control requires the fingers be spread so that as much of the ball as possible is contacted. The ball is *placed* instead of hit (Figure 7.6). The ideal tip looks like a full-blown spike attempt from the first step to ball contact. Blockers duck and defensive players sit back and cover up. Then, the ball is softly dropped in a gaping hole, making the opposing players glare at each other, implying it wasn't *their* responsibility.

Often the tip is used because the hitter does not make himself or herself available to approach, he or she fears being blocked, or the set is bad. These things happen but are not the best reasons to use the tip.

Figure 7.6
Tipping

Roll, or Half-speed, Shot

The roll shot, another change-up, is remarkably like the spiking motion with a *loose wrist* and *relaxed hand,* but the whip velocity of the arm is slowed down. This controlled motion is often used when a player cannot jump and hit but must get the ball over the net. The receiving team of this shot refers to it as a *down ball.* In other words, the ball is coming on a flat trajectory with topspin but is too slow for blocking. The block stays down. Like the tip, this shot can be effective as long as it is tactically interspersed with the "heat."

Setter Dump

A front-row setter is a legal front-row attacker. If the setter continually jump sets, he or she is always a threat to attack. A big, left-handed setter such as Jeff Stork

(U.S. Men's Team, 1988 Olympic gold medalist) can deliver big swings that smoke. Most right-handed setters become deft enough with their left hands to jump with ball-shaped hands ready to set, then drop the right hand (nearest the net) and dump the ball with a tipping technique. The continual threat of the setter dump can be very distracting to the opponent's middle blocker and back-row defenders. But like any off-speed attack skills, overuse will lead to easily controlled balls by the opponent.

Shots and Angles

Rapping the ball hard, tipping the ball deftly, or being able to control a half-speed shot must be tempered by the ability to hit holes in the block, to hit sharp and deep angles through seams in the defenses. There are many alleged volleyball players who are impressive in warm-ups, hammering the ball straight down without any resistance or need to adjust to errant ball control. They will see how high they can bounce the ball off the floor and then look around to see if anyone noticed. (Most of the other warm-up spikers are doing the same thing, so they are only focused on their own attempts.) When the game begins, these warm-up flamethrowers couldn't avoid the block if it were hidden in a closet in a big building. They get stuffed. The harder they hit, the faster the ball lands at their feet. Then, these big guns try to avoid the block by finding open court outside the lines, jeopardizing the safety of passersby. Next, they tip, which is easily read and controlled by the opponents. Finally, the coup de grace—the trip to the vacant seat on the bench. And it all started with a great warm-up. And so it goes. Some form of this scenario plays itself out every day at every level in volleyball.

Do you want to be a great hitter? Find out what works best for you. There are many ways to do this. If you come to the party with great heat, a bludgeon for a hitting arm, a jump that defies gravity, but the playing sense of a mud slide, you will be impressive in warm-ups but wallow in frustration during games. Good hitters have a variety of shots and the practiced instincts to *know when to do what*. The ability to adjust the attack to the situation is the most important hitting skill. When you are practicing hitting, work on the shots. Hit them with as much force as you can control.

Line Shot   Be able to hit down the line on each side of the court (Figure 7.7).

Deep Middle Back   Be able to hit anywhere along the back line, through, over, or around the block between the middle back and wing diggers (Figure 7.8).

Classic Crosscourt   This is the most common and comfortable attack angle. Basically, it is the power alley in direct line with and outside the approach angle (Figure 7.9).

Deep Crosscourt Corner   Learn to use all of the opponent's court (Figure 7.10).

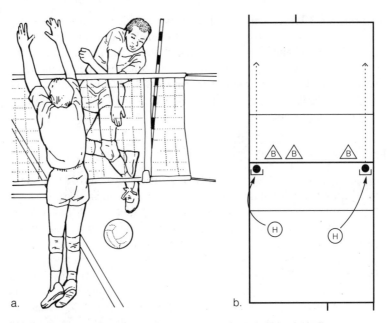

Figure 7.7 Line shot: (a.) the hitter beats the block and hits the ball down the line (notice the player's crossed arms); (b.) this is how a diagram of a line shot would appear.

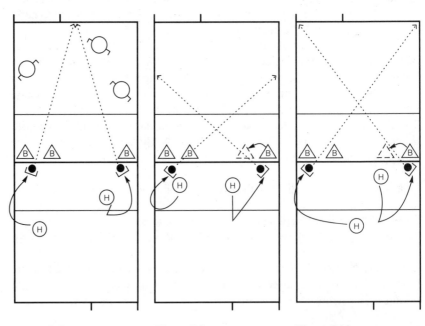

Figure 7.8
Deep middle back

Figure 7.9
Classic crosscourt

Figure 7.10
Deep crosscourt corner

Hard (or Sharp) Angle   This is a difficult shot, requiring a great jump, height, and/or a loose wrist. The ball is hit inside the block and lands inside the opponent's 3-meter line (Figure 7.11).

High Flat   This shot is aimed at the top of the blocker's hands. If you miss, you give up a souvenir to a fan who bought the cheapest ticket in the third deck beyond the end line. If you can skip the ball off the top of the block, the opposing diggers will make a futile attempt to chase the ball into the upper deck. The flat shot is a must for any attacker's arsenal. It is very effective on deep sets and allows for controlled placement. It does not bounce high after hitting the floor, but the resulting side-out or point counts the same as spectacular cannon fire.

Wipe-off   All hitters have to learn the ability to recognize when a set is too tight and the block has closed down all seams. The hitter must then try to hit the ball off the block into an unplayable area. It can be done in one of two ways: if there is simultaneous contact, the spiker pushes the ball against the block and then throws it off the blocker's hands; or, if there is a gap between the block and the ball but little opportunity for an angle shot, the hitter must try to hit the ball off the outside hand.

Tap   Another option when confronting a closed block is to poke the ball into the block, get it back from the rebound, pass to your setter, and try again.

Against the Grain   Along with the tap, hitting against the grain may be the most difficult maneuver. Approaching in one direction, you twist during the jump and hit back toward the direction from which you came. It is important, of course, that the ball go into the opponent's court.

These are basic shots and angles. Other options present themselves as a game progresses. After you have mastered the basic mechanics of spiking, practice the many varieties of shots. Certainly, experience the basal animal joy of crushing the ball straight down. But understand that the key is to harness the power and practice the variety of shots.

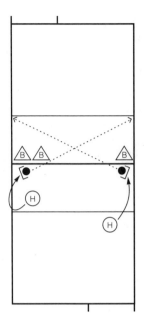

Figure 7.11
Hard angle

BASIC TEAM ATTACK PLAYS

In the final analysis, the attack is one player—the spiker—hitting a ball in the air above the net against the opponent's block and back-row defense. This is *individual attack*. When playing six-player teams, the tactical component that gets most of the attention is *team attack*. A variety of approach routes by each hitter are orchestrated with teammates and combined with different heights and speeds of sets. The team attack relies heavily on consistent, accurate serve receive, so the setter can select any option. The purpose of the mixed attack routes and set variety is to confuse the block, opening up holes and gaps. This confrontation is much like a football team sending downfield several receivers running a variety of predesigned routes against defensive backs. The defensive backs have to wait and see where the receivers are going and react. The quarterback (setter) selects the receiver (spiker) and delivers the pass (set).

After the basic mechanics of hitting and the varieties of shots are mastered, you should explore the tactical team attack skills. Quick sets, play sets, and back-row sets are the basic components of team offensive play. These will be covered more thoroughly in Chapter 12.

Practice Activities

Make good or make tracks.

–Savvy Sayins

Still reading? You shouldn't be. It's time to go do.

Self-bounce and Hit
You need a ball and a net. A partner is preferable to reduce shag time.

ACTION: Bounce the ball on the floor in front of you so that it goes between you and the net and above its top. Take an accelerating approach, adjust to the location of the ball, and hit it as hard and as high as you can control. Your partner, on the other side of the net, retrieves the ball and repeats the action back to you (Figure 7.12).

ADVANTAGES: This activity takes little equipment and personnel. It helps to learn how to adjust to the moving ball. It also aids in learning relative spacial awareness of the ball, net, and opponent's court.

DISADVANTAGES: It is not gamelike, even though some basic adjustments are close.

NOTE: This is much preferable to hitting a ball against a wall. A common method of warming up the arm or teaching an arm swing is hitting a ball against the floor and short hopping the wall so it bounces back. Although this allows for more repetitions, the player is only learning how to hit a ball against a wall, and there is little transferal to the skills of approaching, jumping, and hitting a ball over a net.

Self-toss and Hit
Basically, this is the same as "self-bounce and hit" except that the ball is tossed instead of bounced. It happens quicker and, therefore, requires a quicker adjustment. The toss is more accurate, though, so the adjustment needed is more predictable.

One-on-One
Two players, a ball, a net, and a court are required.

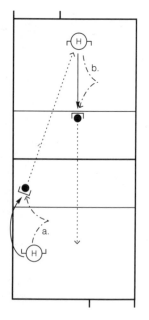

Figure 7.12

Self-bounce and hit

ACTION: The court width and length are arbitrary. Measurements of 3 to 4 meters in width and 9 meters in length from the net to the back line are recommended. The net must be at legal height (7 feet 11⅝ inches, or 2.43 meters, for men, and 7 feet 4⅛ inches, or 2.24 meters, for women . . . nice round numbers, eh?). Each player gets three contacts. One player serves to the other. The receiving player passes to himself or herself, sets, and then hits back to the other player. The game continues as normal volleyball with the exception that each player gets up to three contacts. Regular or rally-point scoring can be used.

ADVANTAGES: There is efficient use of space and simplicity of organization. It is fun. It emphasizes ball handling that balances velocity and control. It encourages the rudiments of tactical placement.

DISADVANTAGES: It does not teach accurate ball-handling deflection angles. One never passes to oneself in team volleyball. It often discourages accelerating approaches with explosive jumps.

Deep-court Exchange

This activity requires a full court, a net, a full bucket of balls, six to fifteen players (a number divisible by three), and one coach (two are preferable). This drill incorporates the skills of ball handling, individual attack, and digging.

ACTION: Three players on each side of the net take up back-row positions. The other waves of three are positioned behind the court to come on after the ball has crossed the net from their respective side to the other. One coach, standing near one of the net standards, begins the play by hitting a ball to one of the three players on his or her side of the net. The receiving player passes the ball to a teammate, who, in turn, sets the ball to either teammate, who then attacks the ball (Figure 7.13). All attacks must be out of the *back row*. (The hitter must take off from behind the 3-meter line.) As soon as the ball crosses the net, the three players on the attacking side step off the court and the next wave steps on.

When a play is terminated, the coach on that side of the net repeats the terminating play until the team controls it and continues the action. For example, a player from team A hits a ball to a line digger on team B. The digger misses the ball. Coach B immediately hits balls at that digger until one is controlled and play continues. If a hitter makes an error, the coach tosses a ball to a player to set to the attacking player until one is successfully hit to the other side of the net. Basically, the deep court exchange is a timed drill but can be played for points.

ADVANTAGES: It is a great team warm-up. It presents many opportunities to respond in gamelike conditions. It is a specific physical training activity. It requires live-fire adjusting movements. Communication is important. Spacial awareness is developed. Peer pressure is realistic. Players love it.

DISADVANTAGES: None.

Most volleyball activities include hitting because it is a terminal contact—the goal of most sequences of play. The games of doubles and triples, described in Chapter 11, are excellent in learning live-fire spiking. It is important to reiterate that the key to learning spiking is to do it under gamelike conditions. All the

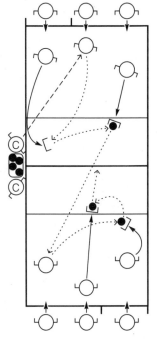

Figure 7.13
Deep-court exchange

components must be practiced together because they are directly related and cannot be separated. You must approach and accelerate, jump with an explosion, hit like a whip. This occurs while dealing with a *moving* ball. By hitting a suspended ball, you only learn how to hit a suspended ball. Practice the motor patterns that are consistent to the total skill.

To test your comprehension of the key elements of attacking, turn to Worksheet 4 at the end of the book.

TROUBLESHOOTING
Attack

Problem	*Solution*
Hit goes too long.	Start your approach later and *accelerate;* contact the ball as high and as far in front of your hitting shoulder as can be controlled (stay *behind the ball*); hit the *top* of the ball with a loose wrist and an open hand and snap.
Problem	*Solution*
Hit goes into net.	Contact the ball as *high* and far in front of your head as can be controlled; keep your hand up after snapping over the ball instead of pulling through; keep your head up; aim for the back line.
Problem	*Solution*
Attack results in a net foul.	Jump *vertically* by pulling your arms through and up; take off on both feet, heels to toes, simultaneously as arms lift up; jump *closer* to point of contact; always be aware of where you and the ball are in relation to the net; if the ball is set tight, swing *parallel* with the net, hitting as much of the ball as is available.
Problem	*Solution*
Shoulder is sore.	Contact the ball as *far and as high* in front of your hitting shoulder as can be controlled; if you are right-handed, make sure your steps are *left, right, left;* lefties step *right, left, right;* contact the ball in line with your body.

Problem	**Solution**
Player cannot hit hard.	Swing your arm loose and *quicker;* hit the ball in line with your body; stay *behind* the ball.
Problem	**Solution**
Player is unable to get a good swing in transition.	Always make yourself *available* when your team is in control of the ball by getting away from the net so that you can approach and the setter can set the ball *between* you and the net.

Block

8

Blocking is the first of two lines of defense. Blocking is a terminal skill that directly leads to one of the four ways to score: service ace, stuff block by the serving team, a successful counterattack after the serving team retrieves the opponent's attack attempt—known as *transition attack,* and receiving-team error. Blocking is the simplest skill to execute technically but the most difficult tactically. It has little intrinsic positive feedback. A blocker can do everything correctly and not even touch the ball. At times it seems futile and is definitely frustrating. Although most good blockers are tall with long arms and big hands, short players can be effective blockers, even if they don't often touch the ball. How? you ask: by always establishing the best position *fronting* the hitter. Every player has to have a thorough knowledge of the mechanics and tactics of single and multiple blocking.

At most levels of play, one of the most important skills is knowing *when not to block.* Effective blocking can turn the tide of games and matches. Likewise, indiscriminate blocking can be the equivalent of shooting yourself in the foot.

Keep in mind that blocking is not a recreational activity. You and your friends may say, Let's go out back and shoot some hoops, or, Let's toss around the football, or, Let's go out and hit a little fungo, or, Let's go play pepper and set some balls; however, it is doubtful anyone has said, Let's go out back and block a few balls. This may be a good way to end a relationship. After all, blocking *is* a terminal contact.

GAME APPLICATION

It is generally thought that offense has the most tactical components. This is probably true at the beginning and intermediate levels of play. At high levels of competitive volleyball, in which game plans become an integral part of matches, much attention is applied to how to stop the opponent's offense. Even at this level, blocking tactics are often secondary to backcourt strategies. The reasons for this seem to be that few people understand blocking tactics and when linked with the difficulties of teaching and learning blocking, these tactics are given cursory attention. However, a basic understanding and execution of blocking tactics can lead to momentum-changing and game-winning points. The satisfaction lies in making the right choice and seeing it bear fruit. Even though there are many complex strategies, just the basics will be covered here.

Three Functions of Blocking

Blocking has three functions:

Figure 8.1
Stuff block

1. The *stuff block* is one of the four ways of scoring in volleyball and is accomplished by stuffing the opponent's attack when your team is serving (Figure 8.1). This is a terminal contact magnified. If you are in the opponent's house, the partisan crowd, anticipating a thunderous spike, will go silent when the stuffed ball hits the home floor. A good stuff—also known as a *roof* or *putting a hat on it*—can make a normally great hitter feel like he or she is playing in a one-seat outhouse. Nothing can shake up a good hitter like getting stuffed.

2. A *control block,* also known as a *touch block,* is where the blocking player(s) deflects an attacked ball so that it is playable by teammates (Figure 8.2). In

Figure 8.2   Control block

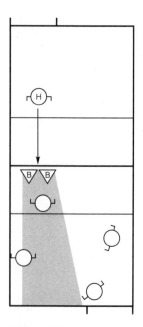

Figure 8.3
Zone block

a true control block, the ball can be retrieved so that the blocking team can mount a counterattack, or transition attack, which is another of the four ways to score.

Over the course of a match, consistent control blocking can take a devastating toll. Hitters like to see their spike attempts careen off the opponent's floor. If they are continually getting touched by the blockers, spikers will start to modify their shots and setters will make other choices. Then come the hitting errors.

3. A *zone block* occurs when the blocker(s) assumes a position so that the hitter must hit in a specific backcourt area to avoid being blocked (Figure 8.3). In other words, the block takes away an area, or zone, and forces the hitter to channel the ball into the defending team's backcourt strength or to try to hit an uncomfortable shot.

Historically, coaches have tried to teach these three functions separately, using different mechanical skills. This increased the frustration in learning the complicated skill of blocking in general. After much thought, consultation, and study, Doug Beal (1984 U.S. Olympic gold medal–winning coach) proposed that if blockers go for a stuff every time, the other functions will happen naturally. Obviously, a stuff block is preferable because it is a terminal contact. In order to get a stuff, blockers must be in good position. Therefore, if the block is stable, balanced, and going vertical, it forms a natural zone block, and the back-row players can easily get into the available angles. If the hitter elects to spike at the block, he or she is likely to get stuffed or controlled. Otherwise, the hitter has four options: hit into the available zone, hit out of bounds, hit into the net, or tip. The defensive team will gladly take any of these options.

The hand position does not change in any of the three functions. A control block will result if the attacked ball is hit high and hard. The hands will be knocked back, naturally deflecting the ball up and back. There are occasions when blockers are fooled by the opponent, and they just try for a touch and reach with their hands back; this is an instinctive reaction that is borne in experience. However, you should always go for the stuff. The other functions will occur if the first does not.

Knowing When Not to Block

There is tendency for beginning-to-intermediate players to block without discretion. They do it because it is part of the game, with little regard for the real threat of the attack. An important analytical skill is being able to determine the capability of the opponent to spike in any given play. You must be able to process this information as each play unfolds. Who is the hitter? Is he or she short, tall, a lefty? What kind of jump does he or she have? Can this hitter hit the line? . . . ever? What kind of approach does she or he have? What about the setter? Can he or she even get the ball to the hitter? Is the set too low, too deep, inside or outside? (In other words, is it hittable?) Basically, you need to make a split-second assessment of what kind of set is delivered and match that information with what you know about the hitter's position and capabilities.

It is easier said than done. Remember, you have at least one other teammate blocking with you. Make an independent decision and you might leave your teammate hanging. A risk of not blocking is misreading what the attacker can do and having that player blast one, putting your back-row defenders at peril.

However, the greatest risk is in what can be referred to as *blocking atrocities*. There are many potential blocking problems. The most common are:

- *Net or centerline violations due to poor balance and stability*. For example, the hitter is under the ball and can't get a good swing. He or she takes a cut at it anyway and drives it into the rafters. However, you attempt to block, having no prayer of touching the ball, and come down into the net. Point, attacker.

- *Attempting to block a ball that has little chance of being effectively hit*. For example, the set is tight, snuggling next to the antenna. You reach out to block. The hitter does not have a good swing but can slap the ball into your outstretched hands. The ball careens off your hand, then hits the antenna. Point, attacker.

- *Fading outside when jumping*. For example, the ball is set wide. You jump to block, fading to the outside with the ball. The hitter does not have a good approach but cuffs the ball, ricocheting it off your inside hand and away from the crosscourt digger who had an easy angle. Point. Not yours. And so it goes.

The overriding keys to consistent blocking are knowing when to block and using good, basic mechanics in the effort.

MECHANICS

It is very difficult to separate the mechanics from the tactics of blocking because of the unfolding variables of play. However, there are some basic skill keys:

1. Move with *balance*.
2. *Front* the hitter.
3. Jump with *stability*.
4. *Block low and tight* with big, hard hands

Before any tactics can be employed, basic individual blocking techniques must be learned. Perhaps more than any other skill, blocking intertwines tactics and mechanics. Therefore, understand the tactical relationship of each mechanical component.

Footwork

There are three basic footwork patterns.

Figure 8.4
Ready position

Two Step   The two step is the most basic of the patterns and should be used as often as possible. It is the simplest to execute and allows you to always stay in *balance* when moving and to establish a *stable* base for jumping. The ready position is the same for all footwork patterns. The feet are comfortably at shoulder width. The weight is slightly forward over flexed knees. The back is straight. The hands are relaxed, open, and held in front of and at approximately the same height as the shoulders. The head is up, with the eyes tracking the ball but recording the surrounding action in the periphery (Figure 8.4).

The move is initiated by the foot nearest the direction of intended travel. Keeping the body weight between the feet, step to the position from which you intend to jump. Plant the lead foot hard so that you can convert the explosive lateral movement to a vertical one without fading. The trailing foot is planted comfortably at shoulder width away from the lead (Figure 8.5). The feet should be parallel with the centerline.

There are two common errors in the two-step pattern. There can be a tendency to *step in the bucket,* that is, stepping away from the net with the lead foot. This happens because blockers start too close to the net and feel compelled to step away to avoid hitting the net. Of course, starting too far from the net creates the problem of not getting close enough to get over the net to block. Each player must find a happy medium that allows for parallel movements along the net and the ability to get the hands over to block. The other common error is not establishing a stable prejump base. The trailing foot is often planted too close to the lead foot, creating a small launch platform that usually forces a lower jump that fades in the direction of travel.

Footwork Keys

- Move *parallel* with the net.
- Keep your body weight *between* your feet.

a.   b.

Figure 8.5   Two step

- Establish a prejump base, with your feet at approximately *shoulder width*.
- Always *track* the ball.

Three Step   The three-step pattern is used to cover the most ground. If the set is fast and you have to move 2.5 meters or more to front the hitter, the three-step pattern is the most efficient. The middle blocker is the primary user of this technique. As soon as the path of the set is known, step as fast and as far as you can control with the nearest foot in that direction. The lead foot is planted comfortably. The trailing foot is crossed in front of the lead and planted on, or close to, the takeoff point. The lead foot follows around and is planted with the toes pointing toward the net at about shoulder width from the trailing foot. As in the two step, the body weight remains between the feet. In order to keep compensating movements to a minimum, you should keep your shoulders as parallel to the net as possible when moving. Always track the ball with your eyes. Keep your hands comfortably in front of your shoulders. Your arms should aid in your movements but not at the expense of either fouling the net or having to make a dramatic, flailing swing at a block attempt. Due to the variables in blocking, be as efficient and compact as possible.

The middle blocker has more leniency in movements and postures than the outside blocker. He or she has outside help, more options to consider, and greater distances to travel. Therefore, the middle blocker can reach to close the seam. He or she will occasionally fade into the outside blocker. But nothing is as effective as balanced movements and stable, vertical jumping to block the ball in front of and over your head (Figure 8.6).

Two-step Cross-step   The two-step cross-step is a specialized move to accommodate *stack-blocking* schemes in which one blocker reacts to a misdirection play set and must go around the middle blocker and step toward the net. It is a quick-reaction move that does not cover as much territory as the two- or three-step moves. See where the set is going. Your eyes and head lead toward the direction of the set. Naturally cross-step with the trailing foot to keep your balance. Your lead foot swings around and is planted comfortably at shoulder width, with your toes pointing at the hitter and your body weight between your feet. It is important to get the lead foot all the way around to ensure that you are square with the net (Figure 8.7). Some players prefer this move to the regular two step under any condition. Other players never use the cross-step. Experiment. The bottom line is moving with balance and establishing a stable jumping platform.

Efficient footwork patterns are critical to consistent blocking. It is important to the coordinated movements of two or three blockers. There have been many studies on what is most effective. Several international teams teach the middle blocker to step behind the outside blocker with the first step to prevent stepping on his or her teammate's foot if the reactions are not simultaneous. It is strongly suggested here to make the simplest, most efficient and comfortable moves that accommodate your physical makeup.

Figure 8.6
Stable, vertical jumping

Figure 8.7

Getting the lead foot
around to square up with
the net

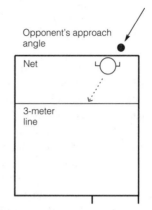

Opponent's approach
angle

Net

3-meter
line

Figure 8.8

Fronting the hitter

Fronting the Hitter

The object of any footwork pattern is to get into a stable jumping position *fronting* the hitter. This basic position is defined as lining up so that the hitter's arm, if it were long enough, would cut from your outside shoulder to your inside heel (Figure 8.8). If you are jumping vertically (and you should be if your footwork is balanced and correct), Figure 8.9 shows what your position should be, relative to the hitter at the moment of contact. Fronting the hitter is the primary responsibility of the outside blocker. Most spikers hit crosscourt. Therefore, fronting means getting into the angle that disrupts the favored shot. Occasionally, the outside blocker shuts off the line, letting the middle blocker jump in the angle. This is often done when three blockers are deployed or the spiker is a notorious line hitter. Basically, the outside blocker fronts the hitter and the middle blocker closes the seam.

Figure 8.9 Proper blocking position at contact

Stable Jump

There has been an ongoing debate about the best blocking jump. Some coaches encourage, and players like, pointing the lead foot toward the outside of the court and sweeping the hands from the outside and up toward the point of contact. Shorter players especially like this jumping technique because they feel they gain more elevation. The trade-off is that the timing of sweeping the arms and hands to the point of contact at the exact moment is difficult at best. It is true that sweep stuffs are spectacular because of the force of movement generated. It is similar to a home-run hitter making solid contact with a letter-high fast ball. Boing! It's gone. The sweep stuff hits the opponent's floor long before the spiker returns. These memories are recounted and legends are perpetuated. Dusty Dvorak, starting setter for the U.S. 1984 Olympic gold-medal team, was a master-sweep outside blocker. He was consistent, predictable, and very effective. Even though the technique is not preferable, his technique was not changed because he got the job done at a high level. In fact, it was Dusty's solo stuff on Brazil's fabled Bernard Rasman that was the final point in the gold-medal match. And so the legend is built.

However, the errors and tactical disruptions usually outweigh the occasional "lights out" block. The sweep jump/block requires great timing, which often opens up seams and gaps the hitter can attack with impunity. The ball often deflects out of play off flailing hands and arms. Defensive players are unsure where to position to dig. Middle blockers are unable to consistently coordinate their takeoff positions.

Elevation is not as important as relative position to and timing at the point of contact. The ball is seldom hit very high over the net (Figure 8.10). A *stable jump*

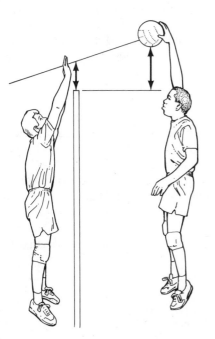

Figure 8.10 Normal net-ball clearance

a.   b.

Figure 8.11   Arm position during jump

Figure 8.12
Hands surrounding the
ball at contact

is the key to good blocking position above the net. To ensure that you will go as vertical as possible, push hard off your outside foot. The angle of flexion at the knees and ankles is determined by body design and relative strength. The arms should be used to gain height but kept in front of the body and as high as possible to minimize the timing in making contact over the net (Figure 8.11).

Arms and Hands

The hands are open, the fingers spread wide. Make your hands as big as possible. The wrists are stiff. When starting to jump, get your hands over the net as soon as possible. The hands go over the net *low and tight*. Remember, the ball will not cross the net very high. *Shoot* your hands at the ball, trying to contact it as far into the opponent's side as possible. *Surround* the ball with big, hard hands (Figure 8.12). Whenever possible, contact the ball in front of and above your head. This gives you maximum leverage and distance on the opponent's side of the court. The further away you reach from your head, the less distance can be penetrated over the net with strength.

Arm- and Hand-Position Keys
- Block with *big, hard hands*.
- Reach your hands *low and tight* over the net.

- *Shoot at* and *surround* the ball.
- *Contact the ball in front of and above your head.*

Timing

It is very difficult to describe the timing of blocking because of the variables involved. Several years ago, the Czechoslovakians did a study to try to identify good timing. Their conclusions are easier to write than to perform: If a set is within a meter of the net, the blocker(s) jumps when the hitter's spiking hand crosses his or her face during the jump; if the ball is set between 2 and 3 meters off the net, the blocker(s) jumps as the hitter is bringing his or her arm forward to the point of contact. These conclusions are general guidelines at best. What if the hitter's hand never crosses the face? What about the hitter that makes contact on the way down from his or her jump? How about the speed of the set? There are too many variables to make timing a cut-and-dry issue. Some players do it naturally; others never get the feel of it. Timing takes practice and lots of playing experience.

Head and Eyes

The eyes are always open, tracking the ball to the point of contact and seeing the hands surround the ball. The head is held still and high. For several years, *piking* was taught, where a player dropped the head at the moment of contact. This was supposed to generate power and allow the player to extend the shoulders and further penetrate the net. The trade-off was that the blocker could not track the ball. Again, decisions must be made as to what takes priority. Seeing the ball while maintaining controlled arm position is most important. Dropping the head leads to flailing arms and fouling the net and losing track of the ball. Like the sweep block, the pike block generates the occasional massive stuff. However, the problems outweigh the successes with the dramatic moves. To be a consistent blocker keep your head up and your eyes on the ball.

Dr. Carl McGown (head coach of Brigham Young University's men's volleyball team and former coach of the U.S. national men's team) is considered one of the world experts in blocking. Along with Marv Dunphy, Carl describes the sequence of blocking in the following keys:

Read and React to the:

1. *Ball* passed in serve receive or transition, evaluating the quality.
2. *Setter*, seeing the ball in the setter's hands and reading the setter's posture and indications of intention.
3. *Ball* in its trajectory line to the apex.
4. *Hitter* approaching the set and seeing the hand make contact.

Blocking requires an aggressive, focused attitude. It must be tempered by making good choices and disciplined mechanics. Often, the inherent frustration can lead to uncontrolled maximum jumps and flailing arms. Blocking must blend an aggressive attitude with shrewd tactics and disciplined, predictable technique. Easier said than done.

Multiple-Player Blocking

Employing two or more players in a block attempt either helps or hinders the play. There is nothing in between. All players involved in a multiple block must have the individual mechanics mastered. Coordination of footwork, position, and timing are the keys to successful multiple blocks. There needs to be one blocker that has the knowledge and experience to select starting and ending positions.

The higher level of play attained, the more important multiple blocking becomes. Mechanics don't change. They must be practiced in coordination with others.

BASIC TACTICS

There are several blocking strategies. As offenses become more sophisticated and consistent, the blocking schemes must be designed accordingly. There are some basic principles and concepts that are applicable to all tactics. *Put the best blockers on the hitter most likely to hit in any given situation.* This simple principle is the one most often overlooked. Most teams line up their net players in the most optimal *offensive* position. Of course, if a good defensive play cannot be made, then premium offensive positioning is a moot point. However, in order to get an offensive transition opportunity, you must make a good defensive play. Establish your strongest *defensive* positions first. Begin with stationing your blockers in their most advantageous positions. This is called *matchup blocking*. Match up your best block against the hitter most likely to hit in any given situation. The deployment in matchup blocking must be made with enough time before the set so that blockers can get into good position but not so soon that the setter can see where all the blockers are located. Scout the opponent's attack tendencies in previous matches to determine who matches up on whom and adjust accordingly to what is occurring in the present match.

Read and React

The most fundamental tactical blocking ploy is directly related to the ability to execute blocking mechanics. After the matchups have been determined, each blocker must track the ball and *read* its velocity and direction out of the setter's hands. The blockers may make slight adjustments within their matchup positions as options are narrowed based on the pass to the setter. They *react* to where the set is going and move accordingly, to the designed routes of the opponent's attack scheme. The blockers only jump with a spiker who is hitting. It is very difficult to discipline yourself not to respond to a fast, well-executed multiple attack. However, it is an important tactical skill to master: Read the ball out of the setter's hands and react to its direction and velocity. Be mindful of who the hitters are and their tendencies and movements, but get to the ball. That is where the hitter must go.

Commit and Stack

Sometimes you run into teams or players that hammer the quick middle very well. They can beat a read because they are on the ball before your blocker can react. Therefore, you must *commit*. Jump with the hitter instead of the ball. Get the hands over the net and into the attack angle before the hitter. However, this will eliminate any chance of getting outside if the ball is set away from the quick hitter. If the block is committing every time, the setter can often get a one-on-one outside. Unless, of course, your team is using *stacks*. Here, one blocker lines up slightly behind and to one side of the committing blocker. While the commit blocker zeros in on the quick hitter, the stack blocker reads and reacts to the direction of the set (Figure 8.13). If the ball is set toward the third blocker, then the stack blocker creates a multiple block. If the set goes to his or her side, it results in a one-on-one situation. The key to the success of commits and stacks is selective use. You don't want the wily setter to pick up predictable tactical schemes.

Dedicate and Invite

Occasionally, you want to *invite* a setter to set to a particular player or location. Do this by either putting a very short blocker in an obvious position or overload all the blockers to one side. The purpose is to influence the setter to set away from a strong hitter or to a weak one.

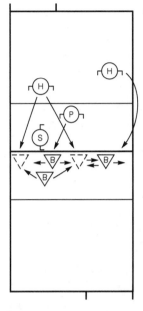

Figure 8.13
Stack block

The sophistication of the back-row attack has put a huge burden on the blocking team. If there are three hitters at the net and one or more attackers threatening out of the back row, the blockers are outnumbered. One response is to *dedicate* a blocker to the dominant hitter. The object is to take away the setter's preferred option.

Tactical Keys

- *Match up* the best blockers on the hitter most likely to hit in any given situation.
- *Read and react* most of the time.
- *Commit and stack* if a team is hurting you in the middle.
- *Invite* the setter to set where you want by overloading or by isolating an obvious weak blocker.
- *Dedicate* a blocker to the primary hitter, especially when there are more attackers than blockers.

Review of Technical Keys

- Be *balanced* when moving.
- *Front* the hitter.

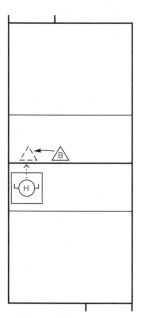

Figure 8.14

Individual blocking drill

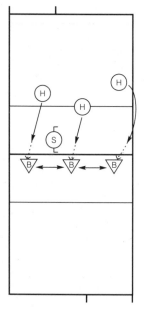

Figure 8.15

Multiple blocking drill

- Be *stable* and *vertical* when jumping.
- Block *low and tight* with big, hard hands.
- *Shoot and surround* the ball above and in front of your head.
- Keep your *head up* and your *eyes open* and track the ball.

Practice Activities

Lightning does the work; thunder gets the credit.

–Savvy Sayins

It was noted in the beginning of the chapter that blocking is not a recreational activity. You cannot go out and block balls without several components being present. You need a net, a setter, a hitter, and several balls, unless you want to spend most of the time chasing down one ball after it is hit. Footwork patterns can be practiced alone, but without real-time, spontaneous reactions, there will be virtually no skill transferal to game situations.

Developing a tactical understanding can be interesting. When watching teams play, take notes on how you would block a particular hitter or how to deploy blockers in the different rotations. Again, there will be very little transferal to the court unless you can put your analysis to the test.

The recommendation here is to practice blocking with attention to keys during any drill that has hitting. Instead of just jogging in warm-ups, go through the blocking footwork patterns. To get a feel of a stuff, have a partner stand on a box on the other side of the net, toss up the ball to simulate a set, and hit the ball. Front your partner; concentrate on a stable, vertical jump; and block the ball, keeping in mind the mechanics keys. Add footwork. Unfortunately, opponents don't stand on boxes hitting balls. However, this exercise will give you many opportunities to respond and practice the mechanics (Figure 8.14).

Nothing is superior to blocking a live hitter. After practicing blocking one hitter, give the setter two options. Then add another blocker and so on (Figure 8.15).

In games, practice the tactical adjustments in every sequence of plays initiated by the serve. Have a coach or trusted teammate quiz you by situation on what you would anticipate and how you would respond.

Blocking can be rewarding as well as frustrating. It can be the determining factor in the outcome of a game and match. A closing thought: The U.S. men's team believes that five stuffs and six control blocks a game are laudable goals. This may not seem like a lot, considering the opportunities presented every game, yet these goals are seldom attained.

To test your comprehension of the key elements of blocking, turn to Worksheet 5 at the end of the book.

TROUBLESHOOTING
Block

Problem

Ball goes between body and net.

Solution

Get your hands *over* the net low and tight; block in front of and above your head; jump *vertically* with stability.

Problem

Ball is hit off your hands.

Solution

Jump vertically; block above your head; make your hands as big and firm as possible; angle your hands to deflect the ball into the opponent's court.

Problem

Hands never touch the ball.

Solution

Front the hitter; execute a stable, vertical jump; keep your *eyes open* and see your hands surround the ball (if you can get your hands over the net, the ball can be blocked); the shorter you are, the more critical the timing is.

Problem

Block results in a net/centerline foul.

Solution

Move to the point of attack with *balance* and jump with *stability;* keep your hands in front of your shoulders and *shoot at and surround* the ball.

Floor Defense

9

Floor defense is where the true competitor shines. It is based on attitude. Even if you have not developed defensive skills but come to the gym with the attitude that no ball is ever going to hit the floor in your area, you are on your way to legendary status. Mastering the various ball-control and pursuit skills will ensure that your focused intensity is parlayed into point- and game-saving opportunities. As the survival skills used in desperation saves are learned, your range of pursuit will widen and the satisfaction of great defensive play will deepen. Without question, floor defense is one of the most enjoyable aspects of volleyball. Digging a hard-driven spike or retrieving a seemingly impossible deflected shot can define how you and your team are willing to compete. Floor defense is one of the unique signatures of volleyball. You are only limited by the physical boundaries of the playing area, not the court lines. If you can get to the ball and keep it from returning to earth, it is playable. An attitude of pursuit—relentless pursuit—is the most important ingredient of great defensive play.

GAME APPLICATION

Floor defense is the second line of defense. If the opponent's attack is not stuffed, the back-row defenders must control whatever gets through. Because there are many things that can happen to the ball in its incoming flight, several tactical maneuvers and related skills must be mastered. The skills of floor defense are intermediate contacts. Unlike passing, floor-defensive skills are often dramatic and can potentially change the momentum of a game. Defense can inspire great transition point-making or point-saving plays.

There are several team defensive tactical schemes. They are designed to take advantage of individual player strengths, to conceal weaknesses, and to respond to the attack style of the opponent. Some team defensive systems are best against an opponent that tips and plays an off-speed game, while others are better suited against a hard-hitting attack. There are many options in between. Team defensive systems will be covered in Chapter 12.

There are tactical considerations for the individual player within any team system. Basically, the team system defines the court area each player is assigned to cover during the opponent's attack. The player's ability to fulfill his or her responsibility depends on three components: mastery of defensive skills, playing within the assigned team-system area, and being able to adjust to the unique conditions of each play.

Each player must be able to apply individual tactics. To achieve success, there is a standard sequence of defense that must occur on each play.

Sequence of Defense

1. *Establish floor position.* A player's general area of responsibility is specified by the team defensive system and, within limitations, modified by the unfolding play. Each player must be able to assess where and how hard the ball can be hit. Analyze the options available to the opponent's setter by being aware of his or her ability to deliver accurately. Know the hitter's preferred shots and situational tendencies. For example, how does any given hitter respond after being stuffed, making an error, coming in cold off the bench, in a close game? Assess the set's location and the spiker's relative ability to hit it. What is the status of your block? Are they fading? Are there gaps? Is there one short blocker and one tall blocker? All this information must be analyzed instantaneously and floor positions adjusted accordingly (Figure 9.1). This is commonly known as *anticipation.*

   It often is said that great defensive players are quick and have great reactions. This is not necessarily true. This phase of defense requires the ability to focus on the unfolding situation of each play and choose the right floor position. You can be a lumbering, out-of-shape player and locate the right floor position every time even before the ball is hit. If you are not in possession of great quickness, strength, or reactions, be a successful defender by mastering this phase.

2. *Establish body position.* Now defense goes from cerebral to physical. After determining where the ball is going to be hit, physically position yourself to contact the ball with control. A basic principle of good defense is to always be *on help*—a body position that establishes the feet pointed toward the middle of the court, where the ball can be played by teammates. If you are facing a hard-hitting attacker down the line or in a sharp crosscourt angle, there is no time to modify the rebound angle and redirect the ball. Oftentimes the hard-driven ball is returned to the attacking team for another swing. The uninformed will yell, Nice dig! However, a "nice dig" is one that teammates can turn into a counterattack. Position yourself to get the ball to friendly help, not back to the opposition or, worse, the souvenir-hunting fans.

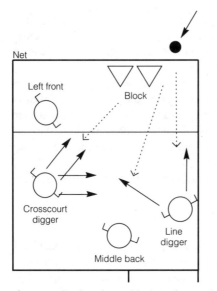

Figure 9.1 Establishing floor position

Get low, be stable, lean forward, and *be stopped.* The basic ready position is assumed after floor position has been established and just prior to the opposing spiker's hitting the ball. The low position is not comfortable over long periods of time. Use the *teeter-totter* method: When the spiker goes up, you go down. If the block doesn't deflect the ball or the spiker doesn't hit some radical shot, the ball should come right down the teeter-totter into your waiting arms. Those waiting arms should be slightly bent at the elbows with the palms up. The keys to establishing a precontact position are to get low and keep your palms up (Figure 9.2).

3. *Prepare to retrieve the ball.* The first two stages of defense are played *before* the ball is struck by the spiker. If you are to have a chance at a controlled retrieval, successfully execute the first two phases. You cannot control what the hitter is going to do with the ball or how your blockers are deploying, so don't worry about these things; however, *do* focus on what you can control—the positional components.

4. *Retrieve the ball.* Commonly referred to as *digging,* the retrieval phase of defense is the response to the final wrinkle of the unfolding play. Digging usually refers to the retrieval of hard-hit shots. The ball is played close to the floor and scooped up. The classic position is similar to forearm passing. The basic principle of retrieval is: *Use the simplest skill required to make a controlled play.* Many players are considered great defensive athletes because they make spectacular saves. At some point in their careers, however, they cross the line of discretion. They receive so many ego-inflating accolades when making gymnastic retrievals that they begin to contort even in the most routine situations. They attempt to make defensive techniques into an art form. These digging artists lose sight of what the defense is trying to accomplish—creating transitional opportunities. The truly great defensive players get the job done consistently using the simplest, most controllable skill.

Figure 9.2   Precontact body position

MECHANICS

There are several skills required to play defense. They can be divided into contact skills and movement skills. There are some general learning keys that apply to each skill:

Learning Keys

- *Attitude*. There is no skill that requires more focus of attitude than floor defense. To learn any of the skills, be willing to go after anything that hasn't rolled to a stop.
- *Low posture*. When the hitter goes up, you go down (the teeter-totter effect). All defensive skills begin from a low posture.
- *Getting Stopped*. When the ball is being hit, you must be stopped.
- *Leaning toward the attacker*. Keep your head up and your back straight.
- *Palms up*. Remember, try to dig the ball in front of you.

All of the movement and contact skills start from these basic keys.

Contact Skills

Remember to use the skill that is most appropriate to the situation. Work hard to position yourself to use the simplest and most effective skill.

Standard Forearm Pass   This skill should be employed often (see Figure 9.3 and Chapter 5). However, if the ball is really smacked and you are relatively close to the net, the rebound angle will deflect the ball back over the net.

J Stroke   Canoeists reading this book are thinking, Say! I know this skill! Probably not, unless you have intermingled paddling and digging. The *J* stroke is a modified forearm-pass position, where the wrists are still together but the thumbs are pointed up and the elbows are bent enough to accommodate the trajec-

Figure 9.3 Forearm pass

Figure 9.4
J stroke

tory of the incoming ball (Figure 9.4). The arms are moved only enough to get the ball up into a playable position. The harder the incoming ball, the less need for arm movement. The *J* stroke is a scooping movement and can be used anywhere from waist height to the floor. In every situation, it is initiated by turning the thumbs up. The object is to either take a hard-driven spike and divert the flatter, incoming trajectory to a more vertical, outgoing path to keep the ball playable on the friendly side of the net or to retrieve a lightly hit ball close to the net so that it, too, remains playable on your side of the net.

Conductor's Wand   This is a one-handed technique that is used only when the two-handed technique is not possible. If you study music, the hand position is similar to that of a heavy-handed orchestra conductor. If you dabble in ranching, the hand position resembles a cowboy wielding a cattle prod (Figure 9.5). This technique should be used only in conjunction with any of the movement skills requiring the player to leave his or her feet. The ball is contacted on the wrist, base of the thumb, and folded fingers. Scoop the ball up, incorporating the wrist and elbow joints. Appropriate shoulder movement is determined by how much force is needed (Figure 9.6). If you can remain on your feet, you should never have to

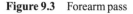

Figure 9.5   Conductor's wand/cattle prod hand position

Figure 9.6   Conductor's wand/cattle prod side slide

Figure 9.7 Flipper

play the ball with one hand below the waist. If you do, you are either being lazy or need to rest.

Flipper   The flipper is used when diving or sprawling if the conductor's wand is not possible or not as comfortable. The ball is played on the back of the hand and snapped up with a reverse flick of the wrist (Figure 9.7). It is effective in an all-out dive, where the ball is about to hit the floor and your only resort is to slide your hand between the ball and the floor and flip it up. It is difficult to employ the elbow joint in the movement.

Pancake   The pancake is an immobile flipper. It is used with a sliding dive or sprawl. The hand is slapped palm down on the floor where the ball will hit. The ball bounces off the back of the hand and remains in play. It is a difficult play to call for an official: Did the ball bounce off the hand or the floor? Your aura of confidence will often sway the judgment. The pancake should only be used when the play dictates that no other arm/hand position will work.

Praying Face Saver   This two-handed technique has a very specialized application. When a ball is hit at you hard and head high and there is no chance to get out of the way (which, of course, is never acceptable unless the ball is going out), it is preferable to make contact with your arms or hands rather than your face. Understand that your face is a legal contact surface. But only boxers with losing records prefer the face to the arms. Bring up your hands, with the wrists together and arms bent at the elbows, to a position where the ball will be contacted on the base of the little fingers and backsides of the wrists (Figure 9.8). The elbows need to be bent enough so that the deflection of the ball will be up and into your court. This positional adjustment will be amazingly natural as your survival instinct takes over.

Knuckler   This one-handed skill is used to punch up a ball that is deflected off the block and is going deep over your head. You don't have time to turn and

Figure 9.8
Praying face saver

Figure 9.9
Knuckler

pursue. Stand high or jump to intercept and redirect the ball vertically so that a teammate can get to it. Another situation requiring the knuckler is a ball close to the net. If a ball is going rapidly into or over the net and there is no room or time to establish a good overhead- or forearm-pass posture, punch the ball up and away from the net for a teammate to play. The fingers are rolled up so that the tips touch the top of the palm. The wrist is cocked so that the ball can be played off the heel of the hand. The elbow is bent and below the hand so that a vertical shot-putting motion can be used (Figure 9.9). It is an amazingly accurate technique. Don't make it a habit, however, because a gaff in a routine situation will be obvious and scorned.

Movement Skills

A simple noise test will let you know if teammates are correctly executing any of the defensive movements requiring body contact with the floor. If it sounds like a load of lumber spilling off a flat bed, the skills are not being properly executed. The following descriptions of defensive-movement techniques will illustrate methods of pursuing the ball anywhere with minimal worry of winding up maimed. These are designed to harness the aggressive-pursuit attitude and allow the competitive player to come back and play another day.

The object of the desperation save or pursuit skills is to be able to hit the floor quietly. That is, to slide and roll on the smooth, rounded, cushioned parts of the body. The corners of the anatomy should seldom contact the floor. These include the toes, ankles, knees, pelvis or hip points, elbows, wrists, fingers, chin, and corners of the head. You may pick up some floor burns and lose a little skin, but you won't be mangling joints and bones.

Standard Forearm-Pass Posture (Digging)   This basic position is described in Chapter 5. The standard forearm-pass posture should be used as much as possible. It can be if you establish good floor position relative to the block and the attacker. This technique is the most common representation of *digging*. One modification to the forearm posture is a wider, lower posture in response to a sharp, angled hard hit. The weight is forward, with the back straight, head up, and eyes focused on the hitting hand contacting the ball. The arms and hands are in front of the knees, the elbows are flexed, and the *palms are up* in the precontact position. The body and appendages are ready to make adjustments quickly. This is the classic digging posture and is best for controlling the hard-driven shot. The ball is contacted on the wrists and forearms between the knees and below the waist. A *J* stroke is the most common contact skill to control the speed and trajectory of the incoming ball.

Keep in mind that things don't always turn out the way they are designed by picture and word. Therefore, play the ball where it is. What is described here represents the *optimal* position. Use this technique as much as possible.

Collapse   "Collapse" is not the kind of terminology one likes to associate with any competitive, aggressive activity. However, the following technique is, in fact,

Figure 9.10 Collapse

a collapse to get the body behind the incoming, hard spike and cushion the impact to modify the outgoing pass. Make every effort to keep the ball between the centerline of your body and the target. Arrive before the ball, and play it with two arms/hands in front of you. Try to keep the incoming shot between your knees. If a ball is hit within a meter of either side of your floor position, step with the nearest foot to keep the ball in your body's centerline. This move usually requires a significant, lateral stretch and will naturally put you low to the floor. It is a quick move; reacting to the incoming shot creates momentum that will cause you to sit over the heel of the lead foot. It is important to keep the lead knee up, pointing toward the target. A common result of the collapse is banging the side of the lead knee to the floor. Concentrate on turning toward the target as you make ball contact. After the dig is completed, you will be sitting over the lead heel and rocking on a crescent shaped back. Keep your head tucked or you will hit those corners. The arm motion required to pass the ball to the target will depend on the trajectory and velocity of the incoming hit. Sometimes you will have to move your arms toward the target; at other times you will actually absorb the shot to keep the ball on your side of the net. Look at Figure 9.10, and try the collapse without the ball. It is easy and, in fact, a good way to stretch your back.

Roll This pursuit skill has many varieties. It is a skill that coaches have studied, analyzed, modified, and philosophized. Many coaches will say that their interpretation is the best, that it is the quickest, most efficient, easiest to control, and safest. However, when exploring this technique, remember the primary objectives: to keep the ball playable so that your teammates can control it; to pursue the ball anywhere, contact it, and not get hurt; and to make a play and to get back quickly into the continuing action. No variety of the roll has been demonstrated to be vastly superior to any other, because each situation requires modification. Try them all and find out what fits you best. There is one constant with each variation: You must be able to roll to all points of the compass and be able to use either arm. There are two basic rolls: the shoulder roll and the barrel roll.

Shoulder roll This is the original rolling skill. It was popularized by the Japanese in the early 1960s. The volleyball version was adapted from the judo

Figure 9.11 Shoulder roll

shoulder roll. As always, the object is to take the necessary steps to get to the point of contact before the ball arrives. Try to get the ball in the centerline of your body line. When the ball is deflected by the block or tipped outside of your floor position into an open area and you cannot get behind it, play the ball outside the centerline of your body line. The ball must be contacted with the conductor's-wand technique just before it hits the floor. The momentum of the effort will force you close to the floor. The movement required to get the ball up will cause a twisting motion. The resulting follow-through will throw the feet over the opposite shoulder. Keep your chin tucked so that you don't hit your head (Figure 9.11). Naturally return to the feet in a balanced, stable position and get ready for the next action. The criticism of the shoulder roll is that it forces the defender to take his or her eyes off the ball, and it is difficult to master the skill to the off-hand side. The shoulder roll can also be used going forward.

Barrel Roll   This technique is a spin-off of the shoulder roll. Try to get to the ball so that you can play it with both arms. If you can't, use the conductor's-wand technique and scoop the ball up before it hits the floor. Momentum carries you beyond the point of contact, so you roll from the lead shoulder directly to the trailing shoulder. Floor contact is on the upper back. Curl your body loosely so that your back is rounded, chin is tucked, and knees are bent. Return to your feet in a balanced, stable position facing the action. The advantages of the barrel roll are that it is simpler mechanically and you never have to take your eyes off the ball during the ensuing play. Traditionalists may criticize the barrel roll, claiming that it does not have as much range as the shoulder roll. However, the defensive range of any player probably has more to do with his or her athletic ability than with the specific technique employed.

Sprawl   This is a front collapse. It should be used as a last-resort play. It often is used as a token effort. It is a necessary move in certain situations. For example: A spiker has pummeled a particular shot time and again and you have anticipated another blast. The savvy hitter, however, changes up with a deceptive move and tips the ball in front of you. You have shifted slightly to your heels (which you really should not do) and do not have time to take a step to the point of contact. You get between the ball and the floor as quickly as possible. Another example: You are prepared for another rocket and the block deflects the ball, slowing it up. Again, you have no time to step to the ball and must hit the deck to get a hand under the ball. Two arms are used for close-in work and a pancake is used in extended efforts. Properly executed, the knees will contact the floor but quietly.

The sprawl is a legitimate technique. Unfortunately, it is applied too often. It encourages going to the knees and elbows and discourages trying to move the feet to the point of contact. It is a natural, reactive move that needs little attention if the collapse, roll, and dive are mastered.

Dive   This skill gives you the most range. Your confidence in pursuing any ball will soar when you know you can sprint to the point of contact and—if a timely arrival is not possible to dig the ball—first, extend, making a controlled contact with the cattle prod, flipper, pancake, or two-handed scoop, second, follow through with a dive, and third, live to play another play. It can be a dangerous skill if it is not properly executed. Take time to learn it. It requires good upper-body strength, particularly in the arms, chest, and shoulders. It can be hard on weak lower backs.

Many women's coaches do not teach the dive because of these potential drawbacks. It is often said that women and girls are not strong enough to perform the dive. However, this belief is incorrect and implies that women and girls cannot develop strength. Every human being can improve his or her strength. If you want to learn this valuable skill, do push-ups every day. Do back exercises and abdominal work. Get in the weight room. Find a good weight-training instructor, design a good program, and have at it. Woman or man, *never* let someone put limitations on what can be done by implying that you are not strong enough. Get stronger through consistent, well-supervised training.

Diving can occur to any point of the compass and be used in two basic ways: It can be used in the same situation as the sprawl but will give you more range; or it can be the extension of an all-out sprint for a ball when you are running out of time and air. It is a follow-through move. Play the ball off one hand near the floor. The feet are higher than the head, and the head is higher than the hand contacting the ball. Contact the floor mostly on your torso from the diaphragm to the waist. Keep your chin up and arch your back (Figure 9.12). Sometimes you have to extend so far out to touch the ball that you slide on the forearm and side of the contact hand.

There are variations to the classic dive. For example, the *side slide* (see Figure 9.6) is a combination of a roll and a dive. During close-in work, it is difficult to distinguish between a sprawl and a dive.

Figure 9.12 Dive

Floor Defense Principles and Objectives

- Use the simplest skill to play the ball.
- Make every effort to arrive at the point of contact before the ball.
- Make every effort to keep the ball between you and teammates.
- Master the skills of floor contact to increase your range to pursue the ball without fear of getting hurt.

The floor-survival skills are essential for extending your ability to play this exciting part of volleyball. Each situation provides a challenge to play the ball with control. And that is the object. If you look pretty performing each move but can't dig a hole let alone a ball, then you are missing the point of this chapter.

Learning Keys

- Establish *floor position*.
- Get *stopped*.
- Assume a *low,* balanced, forward-leaning posture.
- Keep your *palms up* and your elbows bent.

Practice Activities

If you have a hill to climb, waitin' won't make it smaller.

  –Savvy Sayins

Did you mess around with these skills when you looked at the pictures? You should have. Reading about it won't get it done. Do them slowly without a ball. It is important to explore these moves with intensity tempered by patience and caution. If your enthusiasm overrides your common sense, attempting dives and rolls at full throttle the first time out can be hazardous to your health. Proceed only as fast as you can control. Most skills should be learned in the context of the game as soon as possible; however, the pursuit skills should be learned separately before adding a ball because of the potential risks.

Learning Progressions for Pursuit Skills

The following descriptions are recommended learning progressions for the collapse, roll, sprawl, and dive.

Collapse
Assume a low, ready position. Step as far as possible to one side. Sit down over the heel of the lead foot and rock back. Keep the knees up. Don't touch the floor with the hands. Repeat to the other side.

Roll
Basically, the roll is an extension of the collapse with enough momentum to carry you over your shoulders and back to your feet. Try the shoulder roll and barrel roll. Try them to your favored side first. Move as fast as you can control. Repeat until comfortable to both sides.

Sprawl
You learned this skill at a very young age. It is time to relearn it. Do it a few times without a ball and then have a partner toss balls easily so that you can try the conductor's wand, the pancake, and the flipper.

Dive
More than any other skill, diving requires the most careful development. Begin by getting down on both knees. Find a scuff mark, board line, or stain in front of you on the floor. Adjust so that the mark is 4 to 6 feet away. Keep your knees bent while you push off your toes, and slide on your torso and reach for the mark. Make sure you keep your chin up. Next, get down on one knee. Adjust so that the mark is 8 to 11 feet away. Rock over the up knee, touching your chest to that knee, and reach for the mark and slide over it. Keep your knees bent and your chin and heels up, creating an arch in your back. Be low to the floor but airborne in this exercise. Next, assume a defensive ready position and establish a floor mark beyond 8 feet.

Dive for it from a low position. Keep your knees bent, your heels above the level of your head, and your chin up. Contact the floor with both hands and slide through, arching your back and making initial torso contact on your diaphragm. Finally, dive off a run. The takeoff position is the same as when you knelt on one knee. Your chest is at knee level when you launch into your dive. *Keep your chin up*.

As you get comfortable with these pursuit skills, use them as part of your warmup. Intermingle them, going only as fast as you can control. When you can hit the floor without concern, add a ball to your practice and use the various contact skills previously described. You will soon discover which of the techniques suit you best.

Digging Activities

Pepper   There are several defensive ball-control activities that come under the heading *pepper*. A few are described below.

Two-Player Control

Two players with one ball face each other 15 to 20 feet apart. The action begins with player A setting the ball to player B and assuming a defensive posture. Player B hits the ball as hard as he or she can control so that the point of contact is between the knees and ankles of Player A. Player A digs the ball back to B, who then sets the ball back to A. Player A now hits to player B. The object is to keep the ball in play as long as possible. A variation has one player hitting every ball that is dug by the partner instead of setting back. After a preset number of repetitions or specified block of time, the players switch roles.

ADVANTAGES: The logistics are simple. It is a good warm-up, emphasizing ball control.

DISADVANTAGES: It is not gamelike. Often, the hitting player does not hit with enough control or heat.

Over-the-Net Pepper

Four or six players, a ball, a court, and a net are required. The court dimensions are 9 meters long by 3 meters wide. The court dimensions can be adjusted to the range and skill of the players. The action begins with one player on team A tossing or serving the ball to team B. Team B passes, sets, and hits to team A. They dig and return in kind. The object is digging control, so the hitters should hit at the defender. The players rotate each time the ball goes over the net to the other team. Player 1 digs the ball to player 2, who sets back to player 1, who hits as hard as he or she can control to the other team (Figure 9.13). Player 1 then becomes the setter and player 2 goes back to dig the next shot. If there are three players, one player is off the court and rotates into the setting position while the digger rotates out.

ADVANTAGES: It is gamelike. It incorporates all basic volleyball skills in realistic situations. It requires communication.

DISADVANTAGES: None worth noting.

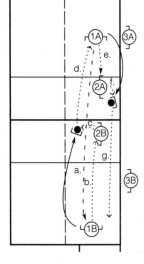

Figure 9.13

Over-the-net pepper

Triad Pepper

Three players and one ball are needed. Player A is the hitter, player B is the digger, and player C is the target. The digger is facing the net 15 to 20 feet from the hitter and target. The action begins with player C setting the ball to player A. Player A either jumps or stands and hits as hard as he or she can control to player B, who digs to player C, who again sets to A. Player A must hit the ball in the area where the digger is playing. After a block of time or a specified number of repetitions, the players rotate.

ADVANTAGES: It is logistically easy. There is a potential for many repetitions in a short period of time.

DISADVANTAGES: The origination and angle of attack are not realistic.

Coach-Centered Drills

There are several coach-centered drills in which a coach initiates the action and controls the tempo.

Coach on One

This is a classic defensive drill in which the coach hits balls at one player for a specified block of time or until the digger retrieves a preset number of playable balls. The coach controls the difficulty and goals of the drill. It can be very physically demanding depending on how tough the coach decides to be. The coach can be standing on the floor or up on a box hitting the balls across the net to the player. These types of drills require many balls, containers for collection, and several support people to shag dug balls and return them so that the coach can continue the onslaught. Varieties of this type of drilling are limited only by resources and imagination. There can be more than one digger involved as well as setters and hitters.

Deep-Court Exchange

Deep-court exchange is an excellent defensive drill. See Chapter 7 for a full description of this activity.

To test your comprehension of the key elements of floor defense, turn to Worksheet 6 at the end of the book.

TROUBLESHOOTNG
Floor Defense

Problem	*Solution*
Tips hit floor in front of defender.	Be *stopped;* lean *forward* toward the point of attack (keep your knees in front of your toes and your head in front of your knees); keep your arms *loosely bent* at the elbows, with your hands *palms up* in front of your knees; maintain a low posture.

Problem

Dug ball has too low an outgoing trajectory.

Solution

Contact the ball *away* from the torso; Use the *J* stroke by turning your thumbs up and bending your arms at the elbows; contact the ball low and in front of you.

Problem

Ball goes back over net.

Solution

Play *on help;* use the *J* stroke; stay low; cushion the incoming ball with a collapse or "soft arms."

Problem

Player can't control one-hand ball contact to left.

Solution

Practice contacting the ball with the hand/arm *on the side* the play must be made (play a ball to the left with the left arm and a ball to the right with the right arm).

Problem

Chin hits on dive; shoulders hurt.

Solution

Do sets of push-ups everyday; start the dive from a *low position;* dive and *slide,* don't dive and catch; keep your *chin up;* keep your *heels up;* arch your back.
Important: Practice this skill going only as fast as you can control.

Problem

Player is never in the right position.

Solution

Review the sequence of defense: Establish *floor* position (assess what position the block is taking, the attacker's approach and timing, and determine what area of your floor responsibility can be hit and get there); establish *body* position (get low; be stopped; lean toward the point of attack with your palms up); when the ball is *hit,* keep your eyes open and *read* any adjustments the hitter might make (i.e., tip, soft shot, wipe-off); *retrieve* the ball, using the simplest technique needed for control.

Physical Training
for Volleyball

10

This chapter is not intended to be a detailed, scientific presentation on physical training. Although the information in this chapter is based on basic physical-training principles, the objective is to provide some general, usable information written in plain language about the fitness requirements of playing volleyball.

Volleyball can be a very physically demanding sport. It is not dangerous; in fact, there are seldom traumatic injuries. However, there can be many irritating soft-tissue injuries that can curtail participation. Ankle and finger sprains, sore shoulders, bruises, knee wear and tear, and back soreness are common. As your ability to play volleyball develops, you can reduce the potential for these nagging maladies by concentrating on three areas: improving your physical fitness level, efficiently and correctly executing the skills, and having complete body control.

IMPROVING YOUR FITNESS LEVEL

There are many principles governing physical fitness and related training. The objectives of this book are best served by two important principles:

1. *The level of physical fitness of an individual correlates to the capacity to cope with the physical requirements of any athletic activity.* In other words, the better conditioned you are, the easier it is to perform physical activity.

2. *Fitness is specific to any given physical activity.* In other words, if you want to excel at any sport, train your mind and body to play that specific sport.

Every sport has its unique aerobic, anaerobic, strength, power, flexibility, and movement components. An ironman triathlete would be very sore after a bout of extended, intense volleyball play. Likewise, the honed volleyball player would probably be comatose after a triathlon. Healthy, fit, people who participate in an activity for which they haven't specifically trained will certainly do better than those less fit, but they will still suffer soreness and fatigue. Therefore, if you want to be superbly fit to play volleyball, then *practice volleyball-related movements* in your training regimens.

AN AEROBIC BASE

Aerobic means "with oxygen." It is obvious that healthy, efficient muscles must be able to take in, move, and use oxygen. It is a generally accepted axiom that anyone engaging in a vigorous activity needs to be aerobically fit. You should be able to run 1½ miles in 12 minutes or 2 miles in 16 minutes. Run at least 25 to 30 minutes three to five times a week to develop and maintain an aerobic base. An aerobic training effect will occur if you can sustain a heart rate of approximately 80 percent of your anaerobic threshold.

In simple terms, a *training effect* is the phenomenon of increasing aerobic capacity by going beyond your present level of fitness either by increasing the sustained time of effort, the intensity of effort, or a combination of both.

The common formula for determining your *anaerobic threshold* is 220 minus your age. Therefore, if you are 25 years old, your anaerobic threshold heart rate is 195 beats per minute (bpm). Your *aerobic training heart rate* would be 80 percent of 195, or 156 bpm. Sustain a heart rate of 156 bpm for 20 to 25 minutes every workout, three to four times a week, and you will solidify your aerobic base.

An aerobic-base fitness level aids in general fitness requirements for every sport. It increases circulation and helps soft tissues become stronger and more pliable. Be careful, however, not to do too much long-distance training because it could be counterproductive to the physical demands of volleyball, which is primarily anaerobic and explosive. The leg muscles would adapt to the rigors of the long road not to the rapidly shifting movements of volleyball. Do enough aerobic work to develop and maintain an adequate base of fitness; then, get specific.

ANAEROBIC TRAINING

Anaerobic means "without oxygen." When the anaerobic threshold is crossed, the system cannot feed the required oxygen to the muscles fast enough and lactic acid builds up. The muscle groups involved start to burn because the cardiovascular system can't ship the waste out and replace it with good, clean oxygen. Breathing becomes heavy and gasping as the demand for oxygen increases.

The anaerobic threshold can be increased with consistent, intelligent training. Using the *overload principle,* which means putting higher-than-normal physical demands on your body (adding time and distance to your workouts), expands the ability to cope with the rigors of a sport. Generally, if you balance aerobic and anaerobic training schemes within the specific requirements of any given sport, the ability to execute the skills and play the game increases.

Training Keys

- *Patience.* It takes time to get into shape. You cannot hurry the process.

- *Sustained effort.* It is not effective to dabble in fitness. It must be a life-style. It takes approximately the same time to lose your fitness level as it does to gain it.

- *Individual differences.* Training benefits everyone, but in different ways and at different paces, because each person has a unique combination of physiological elements.

- *The point of no return.* When you are training and start to lose form due to fatigue, no matter what the activity, you have gone too far. This occurs more in anaerobic training activities than aerobic activities because of the muscle-fatigue factors. If this occurs, *stop.* Injury is next.

- *Recovery.* In training, recovery is the time the body needs between training bouts in order to effectively execute the requirements of the next effort. It is a necessary part of training.

- *Fuel.* Nutrition is important to a training regimen. Eat balanced meals that contain the necessary complex carbohydrates, protein, and vitamins, and be mindful of cravings for foods high in sugar and fat. You don't need supplements or other miracle additives. Remember, though, with an increased workload, there is a need for increased fuel. Keep this under control and balanced.

This overview of the general components of training is rudimentary. There are volumes of research, theories, training regimens, and opinions on training. You can get so wrapped up in the training that playing is an afterthought. If you are truly interested in the complexities of physical training, spend some time and examine the many books on the areas of interest, including:

Fahey, Thomas D., Paul M. Insel, and Walton T. Roth. *Fit and Well.* Mountain View, CA: Mayfield, 1994

Fahey, Thomas D., and Gayle Hutchinson. *Weight Training for Women.* Mountain View, CA: Mayfield, 1992.

Fahey, Thomas D. *Basic Weight Training.* 2d ed. Mountain View, CA: Mayfield, 1994.

Kusinitz, Ivan, and Morton Fine. *Your Guide to Getting Fit.* 2d ed. Mountain View, CA: Mayfield, 1991.

THE INGREDIENTS OF A VOLLEYBALL TRAINING PROGRAM

The complete training regimen is best described in sequence, as it might occur in a career as well as in a daily session. The importance of an aerobic-base level of fitness has been discussed. It is not specific to volleyball and applies to most sports. The ingredients are: (1) warm-up, (2) aerobic development/maintenance, (3) anaerobic (interval) training, (4) resistance training, (5) skills training, (6) jump training, and (7) cool-down.

These ingredients must be blended. They can all be addressed independently, but most have interrelated components. For example, there are several jump-training activities that involve resistance and anaerobic training and use specific volleyball skills. Likewise, the warm-up should also incorporate movements specific to the execution of volleyball skills.

When reading the following sections, you will need to be familiar with some commonly used training terms:

Exercise. A specific physical movement.

Failure. The inability to move through any given range of motion.

Repetition (or *rep*). One successful execution of a prescribed exercise.

Set. A measured series of repetitions.

Timed set. A set that is specifically measured by time and not by a preset number of repetitions.

Workout. A prescribed number of specific exercises organized in sets with a planned work-to-rest ratio.

Warm-up

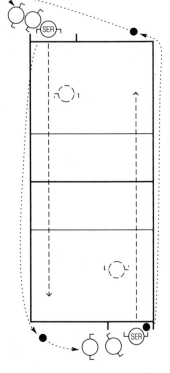

Some form of warm-up should be performed before any training session. You should be ready for action in no more than 12 minutes. The goals of a warm-up include raising the body temperature, respiratory rate, and heart rate, and increasing the flexibility of joints and soft tissue. At the end of the warm-up, you should be mentally prepared to train. The warm-up is a light rehearsal of specific movements that will be used in the upcoming activity. For example, raise the body temperature by playing a game of small-court one-on-one. Jogging intermingled with some easy jumping is a common first phase of warm-up.

"Serve and follow" is another warm-up activity. Serve the ball over the net from a point on the court that doesn't hurt your shoulder and jog after the ball, fetch it, and serve over the net the other way. Several players can participate in a rotating pattern (Figure 10.1). As your arm gets warm, progressively move back until you are serving from behind the end line. As you follow the serve and your legs are getting warm, lift your knees, kick back your heels, sprint four to five steps. In the "three-player shuttle," practice overhead passing and then forearm passing (Figure 10.2). Raising the body temperature and getting the ol' blood flowing should take about 5 minutes.

Next, loosen up the joints and stretch the muscles. Use continuous movements. *Never* bounce stretch. You could spend a good part of a day stretching; therefore, prioritize the areas that need stretching. The ankles, knees, and shoulders will most likely need some loosening. The large muscle groups used in volleyball are important and need attention when stretching: the gastrocnemii (calves); ham-

Figure 10.1
Serve and follow

strings; quadriceps; and back. If you have a slight pull or sore joint, take a little extra time with that area. There are also rehabilitation exercises for injuries that could be categorized as warm-ups, but those are specific and should be designed by a licensed trainer or physiotherapist.

After stretching, crank out some push-ups and sit-ups, do a couple of sets of five to ten block and spike jumps, and begin the main training activity. Your body will tell you when it's warm. You should be sweating lightly. (In hot, humid climates, this may be a deceptive indicator because some people may break out into a heavy sweat just walking into the gym.) You should be breathing heavier than normal, but certainly not gasping. The heart rate should be up in the 125- to 150-bpm range. Remember, each individual is different, so get to know your own level of preparedness.

Aerobic Development/Maintenance

As mentioned earlier, formal aerobic training is not a normal part of volleyball training. If you have a good base, maintain it by doing a 30- to 45-minute aerobic-specific activity three times a week (jogging, hiking, cycling, rowing, and so on).

Anaerobic (Interval) Training

Interval training is at the center of volleyball training. Volleyball is played in intervals. Athletes are in an interval of maximum mental and physical effort from serve to play termination.

Therefore, most training for volleyball is anaerobic in nature, from skill development to jump training. The overload principle needs to be applied to increase the length of intervals for which a player can give maximum effort. Because a long volleyball match is a sequence of intervals of varying lengths, training intervals should be the same to increase endurance. There are some basic formulas to keep in mind when interval training. The *shorter the duration* of the interval, the *higher the intensity* of effort (which is determined by the percentage of the maximum heart rate), the *longer the rest-to-work ratio*. Table 10.1 shows an example of the formula.

Using this formula in an exact form is easy to apply to single-skill event sports such as running, swimming, cross-country skiing, rowing, or paddling. The

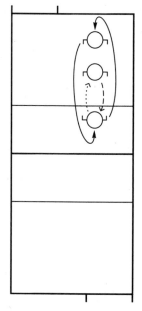

Figure 10.2
Three-player shuttle

TABLE 10.1   Interval Training Formula

Work Duration (in seconds)	Rest Duration (in minutes)	Work/Rest Ratio	Reps	Percentage of Maximum Effort	Percentage of Maximum Heart Rate
60–90	2–3	1:2	8–12	80–90	95
30–60	1.5–3	1:3	15–20	95	100
10–30	.5–1.5	1:3	25+	100	100

athlete can stop and take his or her pulse and compute the percentages. If you were doing a single activity workout, jump training, or running stairs, the above formula could be applied exactly. When training specific volleyball skills, the spirit of the concept can be generally followed, but stopping and taking a heart rate or computing percentages will be replaced by shagging balls, helping teammates, or counting repetitions. Specific applications of interval training are described in the following training areas.

Resistance Training

The most common type of resistance training is weight lifting. There are many different theories and programs in weight training, and it can be very confusing. Consider these important points:

- If a weight-training program is part of your regimen, it must be a year-round part of your life-style. Strength and power gains can be dramatic but only occur over time following a consistently applied program.

- Duplicating specific movements used in volleyball can be done best using free weights (dumbbells and barbells).

- When selecting exercises, keep *balance* in mind. If you are working one muscle that performs in one range of motion, work the muscle that executes the opposite movement. For example, the triceps control the *eccentric* movement (extension) of the forearm, and the biceps control the *concentric* movement (contraction). If you train one of the muscles without equal attention to the other, the arm can be thrown out of balance and lead to injury and, certainly, inefficient movements. This is true for every muscle group.

- When embarking on a weight program, consult with an expert who is aware of weight-training application to all sports. Design an annual program, keeping in mind what activities will be scheduled at any given time during the year. For example, if you are playing in a league, engage in training that is appropriate for a maintenance phase instead of a heavy strength-development phase.

- Concentrate your weight training on the muscle groups that are most often used in volleyball. Duplicate the volleyball related movements of those muscles in weight training.

- Often, there are several exercises that work a specific muscle or muscle group. Use the most specific volleyball-movement exercise. Occasionally change to avoid boredom, but keep *specificity* in mind.

- Lifting free weights is a skill in itself. Incorrect technique can lead to injury or inefficient training effect. Get instruction and supervision. If at all possible, *lift with a partner*.

- Volleyball requires muscular endurance. After a base strength level is attained, focus on the ability to perform over an extended time.

- Volleyball requires explosive power, so include power work in your weight training program.

Strength and Power   Often, people refer to *power* and *strength* interchangeably. Certainly they are related, but they have different meanings. Another word for "strength" is *force*. The ability to move any given weight through a range of motion (ROM) is a function of strength, or force. There is no time element involved, and the distance an object is moved can be considerable but not necessarily significant. If a man lifted the front of a loaded 18 wheeler just a few inches off the pavement, one might exclaim, Whoowee! That fellah is *strong!" But* he might not be powerful. A powerful person can move a significant weight over a prescribed distance quickly.

$$\text{Power} = \text{Force} \times \frac{\text{Distance}}{\text{Time}}$$

For example, a powerful jumper moves his or her body weight from a preloaded squat position through the jump ROM (or distance) very quickly. Watch a great jumper and you will see an accelerating, efficient, quick transfer of weight from a horizontal approach to a vertical lift. There are people who have massive thighs that seem to quiver with strength, yet they couldn't jump over a painted court line. There can be many reasons for this, ranging from lack of technique to body type. But remember, an obviously strong person is not necessarily powerful.

Strength training   The following schedule is a year-round volleyball strength-training program designed by Jerry Simmons and Tom Hille (1984) at the University of Southern California.

Phase I, preliminary (3×/week)

Flexibility	1 each	
Sit-ups	1 set	50
Bench press	2 sets	12–10
Pullovers	1 set	12
Lunges	2 sets	12 each leg
Shoulder press	1 set	12
Leg curl	1 set	12—1 up, 1 down
Tricep	2 sets	12
Bicep	2 sets	12
Wrists	4 ways	Failure
Dip push-ups	1 set	15
Medicine ball	1 set	15
Flexibility	1 each	

At the end of phase I, we do our first testing and evaluation, which includes strength tests, body compositions and dietary analyses. Phase II pre-season is an expansion of phase I in which the athletes increase the sets and intensity during the workouts.

Phase II, pre-season *(3×/week)*

Flexibility	1 each	
Sit-ups	2 sets	50
Bench press	3 sets	10–8–6
Pullovers	3 sets	10–8–6
Lunges	3 sets	12 each leg
Shoulder press	3 sets	10–8–6
Leg curl	2 sets	12–10—1 up, 1 down
Tricep	3 sets	12–10–8
Biceps	3 sets	12–10–8
Wrists	4 ways	Failure
Dip push-ups	2 sets	25
Medicine ball	2 sets	25
Flexibility	1 each	

Phase III, in-season *(circuit program)*

Sit-ups	Shoulder press/flys
Bench (dumbbell)	Pullover
Lunges	Tricep
Lats	Bicep
Ab-adductor	Push-ups
Calf (seated)	Sit-ups
Leg curl	Medicine ball
Leg extension	Wrists

Phase IV, off-season

Monday/Thursday

Warm-up	
Leg press	12–10–8–6–4
Power cleans	10–8–6
Lunges	2 × 10
Leg extension	2 × 10
Hip flexors	2 × 10
Leg curl	10–8–6
Ab-adductors	10–8
Lats	10–8–6
Calves	3 × 12
Buddy sit-ups	30
Sides	30
Buddy sit-ups	30
Sides	30

Tuesday/Friday

Warm-up				
Bench	8–6–4–2–1	Reverse curls	3×8
DB incline	3×8	Wrists	Failure
Shoulder press	8–6–4	Dip push-ups	30
Dips (weighted)	3×8	Hypers	30
Triceps	3×8	Buddy sit-ups	30
Biceps	3×8	Sides	2×30

Conditioning Cycle

Week 1

Monday: $3 \times 7 \times 55$ yds—30-second rest between reps, rest 1½ minutes between sets.

Wednesday: $3 \times 3 \times 220$—rest two minutes between reps, rest 4 minutes between sets.

Thursday: $3 \times 5 \times 120$ yards—rest 1 minute between reps, rest 2 minutes between sets.

Week 2

Monday: $4 \times 6 \times 55$ yds—rest 30 seconds between reps, rest 1½ minute between sets.

Wednesday: $2 \times 4 \times 220$ yards—rest 2 minutes between reps, rest 4 minutes between sets.

Thursday: $3 \times 6 \times 120$ yards—rest 1 minute between reps, rest 2 minutes between sets.

Week 3

Monday: $3 \times 9 \times 55$ yards—rest 30 seconds between reps, rest 1½ minutes between sets.

Wednesday: $3 \times 3 \times 220$ yards—rest 2 minutes between reps, rest 4 minutes between sets.

Thursday: $3 \times 7 \times 120$ yds—rest 1 minute between reps, rest 2 minutes between sets.

Week 4

Monday: $3 \times 10 \times 55$ yards—rest 30 seconds between reps, rest 1½ minutes between sets.

Wednesday: $3 \times 8 \times 120$ yards—rest 1 minute between reps, rest 2 minutes between sets.

Thursday: $3 \times 10 \times 55$ yards—rest 30 seconds between reps, rest 1½ minutes between sets.

Power training   Power training requires using 30 to 60 percent of a maximum single lift. Accelerate the weight as fast as possible fifteen to twenty-five times through the range of motion. Three sets three times a week should be sufficient. The ideal is to keep the weight constant through the ROM. However, the relative weight of a dumbbell or barbell changes with the angle of the arms or legs involved. The Nautilus machines (with the nautilus-shell-shaped gears) are designed to keep the weight constant throughout a ROM. A Cybex machine, often used in rehabilitation therapy, accomplishes the same thing. The trade-off is that specific volleyball movements cannot be duplicated with machines.

For more information on resistance training, contact the National Strength and Conditioning Association, P.O. Box 81410, Lincoln, NE 68501. They do excellent research and publish a superb journal that describes the research and its relationship to specific sports. It is technical in nature and geared to the professional and enthusiast.

Skills Training

Learning and developing the skills of volleyball were covered in Chapters 4 through 9. Practicing these skills alone will improve your physical fitness significantly. If you have no interest or time in any of the other specific training elements, you can benefit greatly from concentrating on the game itself. You will use specific, volleyball-related movements and, at the same time, engage in anaerobic (interval) training. It is important to execute a skill *correctly* each time. If fatigue forces you to compromise the integrity of execution, stop. Train the skills as they will be used in a game.

Increase the intensity, using the overload principle, to lengthen the time you can play at a high level. A sample 2-hour practice that will guarantee a workout and enhance fitness and skill development is included in Appendix A.

Jump Training

Players and coaches of sports in which jumping plays a major role always look for that "magic" that will transform athletes into soaring beings who defy gravity, who can remain airborne to perform the tasks of their trade and leave the spectator in opened-mouth awe. Consider these points on jumping:

- Anyone can increase his or her ability to jump.
- The potential to increase a jump is different among individuals due to several physiological factors, ranging from composition of muscle fiber to skeletal structure.
- There is no such thing as "hang time." It is an illusion. You go up, you come down. You cannot hang around. High jumpers are simply in the air longer than others.

- Do you want to jump higher? Then *jump*. A lot. Use the jumps you will use in volleyball: block jumps and spike jumps.
- The "in" jargon in jumping is to talk about one's *vertical* like it was a car or an attractive physical attribute: Billie Sue has a great vertical! A vertical refers to the height a person can get his or her feet off the floor when jumping. When players get together and discuss verticals, they will almost always embellish the facts: Michael J. goes 41 on his vertical. Yeah? Well the Doctor went forty-*five* in his prime.

  The most important measurement in jumping as it pertains to sport is how high a player can *touch*. Obviously, the standing reach may be the most important practical element in jumping. A shorter player may "fly" and touch 11 feet, yet a taller player may not get his feet as high off the floor but touch 11 feet 4 inches. Shorter players get tired, but tall players never get shorter.
- The higher you can jump, the easier it is to perform the skills above the net.

It can be discouraging to shorter players who train hard to see a taller player be able to spike or block better simply because they are taller. However, as in life, we should concern ourselves with the things that we *can* control rather than those that we can't. Often, shorter players make up for their lack of net dominance with great back-row plays, where the ability to grovel along the floor is the advantage.

The goals of jump training are to improve technique (balance, timing, body control, and so on), power, and endurance. Listed below are the principles of jump training:

- Every jump is a maximum effort.
- Every jump or related exercise must be executed correctly.
- Every jump landing must be cushioned and balanced prior to the next jump.
- A set of exercises should last no less than 15 seconds and no more than 30.
- The work/rest ratio between sets should be 3:1 (for example, 30-second sets require 90-second rest periods).
- The rest period between exercises should last as long as the set and rest times combined (for example, 3 sets of 15 seconds each plus 90 total seconds of rest between sets equals 2 minutes and 15 seconds, or the amount of rest between this exercise and the next).

Table 10.2 outlines the various exercises used in jump training. The first group listed is *plyometrics;* these exercises are characterized by powerful muscular contractions in response to rapid, dynamic loading, or stretching, of the involved muscles. See the section titled "Low-Cost, Easily Found Training Tools" for information about training devices referred to in Table 10.2.

Session Formula   Depending on the level of your physical condition, choose four to six exercises. (Every other workout should include one of the exercises

TABLE 10.2 Jump Training Exercises

Jump Exercises	Variations	Resistance
A. Plyometric		
Snake jumping (elastic)	Over-back over Lateral, over-under High knee tucks High, low (vary snake height)	With or without resistance
Jump boxes (stable)	With or without arms One or both legs Staggered boxes Multiheight boxes	With or without resistance
Stairs	One or two stairs at a time One or two legs "Skating" step Hops and sprints	With or without resistance
Hills	Run, jump, bound One or two legs Up and/or down	With or without resistance
Tuck jumps	On a soft mat or the floor	With or without resistance
Cone hops (traffic cones)	Forward, staggered, lateral Back and forth over one or two cones with no hesitation between hops (minimum 5 cones)	With or without resistance
Depth jumps (30–36"-high box)	Step off, land soft (on mat), and jump Step off, land soft, and jump over measured height (elastic snake)	None
Volleyball jumps	Specific approach spike jumps Standing block jumps two-step, three-step, and combination approaches	With or without resistance (weight belt or bicycle tube)
Bench blasts (bleacher or 20"-high box)	Vary arm rhythm	With or without resistance (weight belt or bicycle tube)
B. Supplemental jump-related		
Boards	Line drills, relays, obstacle course	None
Sprints/accelerations	20–40 yds	With or without resistance (weight belt or bicycle tube)

TABLE 10.2 Jump Training Exercises (*continued*)

Jump Exercises	Variations	Resistance
Bands (surgical tubing)	Lateral slow and fast, forward-and-backward shuttles Obstacle course Ankle exercises	None
C. Specific-resistance		
Mini tramp and dumbbells	Maximum jumps to stabilization Quick-repeat jumps	Weight varies (5–40 lbs)
Shadow jumps	On soft mat, either jumps to stabilization or quick-repeat jumps	Weight varies (20–60 lbs)
D. Measurement		
Vertec (commercial jump measure device)	Standing max jumps, spike and block jumps (should be done once a week)	None

from category A. Likewise, every other session should include two to three exercises with resistance.) Alternate hard and easy sessions. A hard session will include four to six exercises with three to five sets, each lasting 20 to 30 seconds. An easy session will include four to six exercises with three to four sets, each lasting 12 to 15 seconds.

Cool-down

The most neglected element of training is the cool-down. When people are finished training hard and are tired, they often just head for the showers. However, a cool-down can reduce future soreness and fatigue by ridding the muscle tissues of the waste products that contribute to these conditions. Easy stretching and massage can continue the necessary circulation and allow the body functions to catch up. It is not a long or a complicated process. The cool-down should last as long as a warm-up period—about 12 minutes. Easy jogging followed by a similar stretching routine as used in a warm-up are effective cool-down activities.

LOW-COST, EASILY FOUND TRAINING TOOLS

A low budget, or no budget, is the mother of invention. Over the years, volleyball training equipment has been created out of available materials. Only recently has there been an effort to manufacture training tools. The following equipment is effective and easy to obtain, construct, and adapt. The stuff is basically unattractive and, thus, not susceptible to theft.

Bicycle Inner Tubes

Go down to your local bike shop and ask if you can rummage around in their garbage for used bicycle inner tubes. Look for skinny ones because mountain bike tubes are too big. Bike tubes can be used in a variety of resistant jump-training activities. Place the tube under the arms and across the chest, with the valve hanging at the small of the back. A partner holds the tube at the valve and resists against the action of the jumper or sprinter (Figure 10.3). A bike tube can also be filled with sand and tied around the waist and used as an inexpensive weight belt.

Car Inner Tubes

Root around and find a car tire inner tube. Avoid big car or truck tubes. Cut it open at the valve, remove the valve, and fill the tube with sand. Tie off and tape the ends so that the sand doesn't leak. This piece of equipment is called a shadow or a seal. It is called a shadow because it stays with you. It is called a seal because, when filled with sand, the inner tube resembles this mammal. Put the shadow over your shoulders like a stole. Keep your back straight by looking up and jump, sprint, or run stairs, hills, or sand dunes.

Boards

Find a 24-inch-long two-by-four and wrap it in a standard gym towel (Figure 10.4). You now are in possession of one of the most feared and notorious pieces of training equipment. *Board* is the formal name. Listen to someone who has just completed a board workout for more colorful and, perhaps, realistic names. Simply lay out a course on the gym floor and, with both hands on the board, push the board as fast as possible through the course (Figure 10.5). A common board repetition is to start at the volleyball court end line, push to the 3-meter line, return to the start, push to the far end line, and finish where you started. It is not easy but is very good for the legs and cardiovascular system. However, if you have a bad back, this exercise could irritate it.

Elastic Snakes

After you have been to the bike shop, car tire center, and lumberyard, hustle on over to a fabric shop. Purchase 20 feet of ¼-inch or ½-inch elastic. It is known as a *snake* because of some of the configurations in which it can be stretched. The heights and distances can be adjusted to the exercise. Exercises can focus on jumping only (jump side to side, Figure 10.6; jump over, back, over; jump high, jump low) or they can combine skills (dive under, jump over).

Figure 10.3

Jump training using a bike inner tube

Figure 10.4

Board

Figure 10.5   Board workout

Figure 10.6   Jump training using an elastic snake

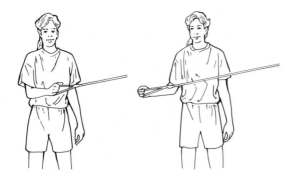

Figure 10.7
Shoulder resistance training using surgical tubing

Figure 10.8
Ankle resistance training using surgical tubing

Surgical Tubing

Head for a medical supply store. Pick up lengths of various sizes of surgical tubing. The thicker the tubing, the more resistance the exercise will provide. A looped length of 3 to 4 feet can be used for gentle work on a sore shoulder or arm. These exercises can be performed to the side (Figure 10.7) or overhead. Make some shorter loops of 8 to 12 inches to work on ankles (Figure 10.8). Regardless of the length, tie the ends of the tubing in a single or double sheet bend or square knot. It is important to periodically check for tears in the tubing because it will snap under stress.

Boxes

Boxes made out of ¾-inch plywood reinforced inside with a two-by-four frame are versatile training devices. They can be used in plyometric exercises and can substitute as platforms for coaches to get above the net to hit balls in certain types of drills. Boxes should range in height from 18 to 36 inches and be 2½ to 3 feet square. Pad the top and edges with indoor-outdoor carpet samples. Jump up, jump down, with or without resistance (Figure 10.9). Use the lower boxes for *bench blasts* (Figure 10.10). **Note:** There is some controversy about the potential injuries to joints in plyometric training. Educate yourself on technique and workload before using these exercises.

To gain maximum benefits from any of these exercises it is very important to know how to cushion your landing by sequentially landing on your toes, then heels, followed by the knees bending to absorb the shock of impact. Coaches tell players to "land quietly," or "land with quiet feet." Also, maintain your balance throughout, especially when you start to fatigue.

Figure 10.9   Jump training using a box

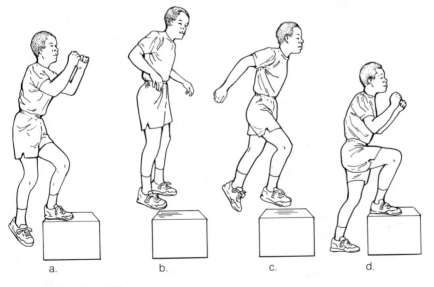

Figure 10.10   Bench blasts

Mats

Gym mats are important to cushion landings in repeat jumping. They also force you to gather and harness your power, reducing the trampoline effect of a good, suspended wood floor. The basic, folding tumbling mats found in virtually every gym in the nation are the best.

Weight Vests and Belts

These are possible to make but much easier to buy. The best vests and belts take various weights. However, belts often come in just one weight, in increments of 6, 8, 10, and 12 pounds. Vests can handle up to 25 pounds. The most important feature to look at in a vest is how the weight can be distributed. It needs to be as snug to the body as possible without hampering breathing. Distribute the weight around the body so that the vest is centered (Figure 10.11).

The devices can be used in all jump-training exercises with the exception of plyometric exercises because of the increased stress on the knees. They can also be used while playing volleyball in the front row. Adjust the weight so that the resistance is appropriate for your strength and fitness level. You need to be able to gauge the appropriate weight according to what feels right.

Traffic Cones

Cones are marketed by some physical education equipment manufacturers, but they are not as good as the real thing. Call up the highway department and see if you can get some used ones (they present a good work image if they are scuffed

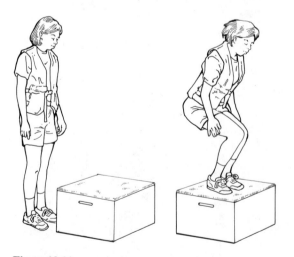

Figure 10.11
Jump training using a snugly-fitting weight vest

up a bit). You can jump over them, sprint or push boards around them, and use them to mark targets for ball-control drills.

Hills

These are usually easy to find and very inexpensive to use. The grades and distances can vary. A good principle to follow is the steeper the climb, the shorter the work distance. If the hills are grassy or consist of soft soil, downhill injuries are lessened. Add resistance or try jumping or skipping with high knees and exaggerated arm swings to intensify the workout.

Stairs

Like hills, stairs are readily available and can be a terrific training device with a variety of exercises: two-stairs-at-a-time sprints; one-stair quick steps; up two, down one as quick as possible; one-foot, one-stair hops; and two-stair, two-foot jumps. Stairs can be hard on people with sore knees, so be aware of what messages your body sends.

Sand

Just playing volleyball on the sand is a fabulous conditioning activity, as anyone who has played on the beach can attest. Design a jump workout on the sand using shadows, bike tubes, or vests, and "rubbery" will be the word to describe the feeling in your legs. Sand is a good medium because it is relatively easy on the joints.

Water

Jump training in water can be very effective. The natural resistance combined with the zero impact on knees, ankles, and the back make water workouts very practical. The major disadvantages are the inconveniences related to using a pool and the fact that water does not allow for work on gamelike jump-approach footwork. If you are rehabilitating a knee, back, or ankle, jump training in water is excellent.

SUMMARY

There are tremendous physical, mental, and social benefits in just playing volleyball. Like any skilled activity—from playing a musical instrument to carpentry to playing a sport—practice is the key to improvement. Improvement means a higher level of execution. A higher level of execution means a wider range of opportunities for enjoyment. Rigorous sport requires specific fitness levels. The higher the fitness level, the easier it is to perform physical skills. This is a valid principle. If you are *specifically* trained for a sport, your general fitness level will be high and your ability to perform specific skills vastly improved. Athletes can get wrapped up in training and forget to play. If that suits them, more power (so to speak) to them. You can see by reading this chapter that a full day could be put into training. If you are really interested in the details of one or all of the examples of training described in these pages, seek out the many books written on each subject. When you decide on a course of training, do so with a partner (or team) who has similar goals and interests. Work with each other. Monitor and motivate each other. You will get greater intensity and enjoyment out of each workout.

Sports are vehicles for enjoying life. The human body is designed for exercise. Sports should be challenging, fun, healthy, social, and satisfying. They should be able to be played for a lifetime in one form or another. So one question remains: Why are you still reading this? Get out there and *play!* Have some fun.

Basic Strategies of Play

11

Volleyball is played in many different ways and venues. Volleyball teams can consist of doubles, triples, fours, and six players. Normal volleyball rules and scoring, with slight variations for the specific games, govern these applications. Coed rule variations in these categories are also described. The traditional environments include playing in gyms on hardwood or composition floors and outdoors on sand or grass. The location as well as coed versions of each category can modify the tactics and are discussed in this chapter. There are, however, some basic principles of play that apply to all variations.

GENERAL PRINCIPLES OF PLAY

Expose your strengths and hide your weaknesses. You must adhere to this principle when playing a competitive game where the object is to win. However, use discretion if you are playing a game for which points define the time of play but the goal is social. Be careful not to offend a player by "hiding" his or her weakness in a social game. Be aware.

Play on help. No matter which variation or system, players should locate themselves so that the ball can be played *between* teammates (help) and/or the net. If players are bunched in the middle of the court or are too close to the net, they will spend too much time and energy chasing the ball away from the field of play.

Develop clear guidelines for 'tweeners. In every variation of volleyball, there are areas between players where the ball is hit (Figure 11.1; **note:** underscored positions designate front-row players). Whose ball is it? One of the dreaded sounds in volleyball is the chorus of two or more players singing out, Yours! Determine who is responsible for court areas in various situations. For example, in doubles, the right-side player may say, I have half and over, meaning that he or

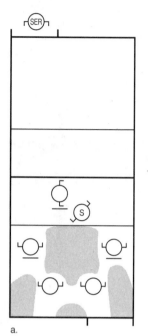

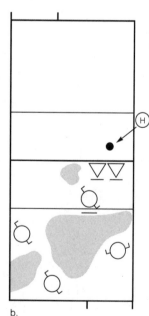

Figure 11.1

'Tweeners: (a.) serve-receive pattern and (b.) defensive pattern.

she will take any ball that hits in the middle of the court and to the right, thus eliminating the middle space between the partners. When four or more are playing, the player in the general area where the ball is coming, who is furthest from but facing the target, is responsible for the next contact. This eliminates players from backing up to play the ball. There are several of these situations that require guidelines to eliminate point-yielding errors.

Design your offense so that you can attack the opponent's weakness. When playing for points and wins, prepare an attack scheme that allows you to go after the opponent's Achilles' heel. A competitive environment requires tactical thinking to determine how best to win. As long as the participants understand and accept the conditions, then exploiting the relative strengths and weaknesses is acceptable, encouraged, and a show of respect. If a social game is being played, remember the focus is the sharing of the experience and fellowship, not tactical maneuvering required to win.

Design your defense to stop the attacker most likely to hit in any given situation. Most volleyball tacticians build their systems of play around offense. The goal is to counterattack. However, if a team cannot block, dig, or control the opponent's attack, countering is a fantasy. Points are scored in volleyball playing defense. You can return fire only after regaining control of the ball. Think about it. It makes sense.

Go to the well until it is dry. When a serve receiver is in trouble, keep serving to him or her. Spike at a weak blocker with impunity. Tip into an open area as long as it works. Force your opponents to adjust to you. Make them react to your relentless assault. Again, however, be aware; be sensitive. If social fellowship and camaraderie are the goals of play, a focused attack on a player can terminate friendly relations. Always play according to the expectations of the day.

Communicate. No matter how light or serious the game is, communication enhances the experience. It should be supportive in nature. There are formal and informal communication systems.

Formal communication includes calling for the ball, outlining attack patterns or blocking matchups, and using hand signals for offensive or defensive adjustments. Preestablished, one-syllable words clearly spoken and heard are common in communicating intentions in each phase of the game. For example, players should always yell *mine* or *ball* prior to playing the ball. Full sentences or multi-syllable words can get lost in the din of poor acoustics. "This here incoming baby is my plum to pick" may describe in colorful terms a serve receiver's intentions but will cause confusion.

Informal communication includes ongoing, positive reinforcement of teammates. Silence often communicates a negative response. Turning one's back on teammates implies disassociation. Rolling one's eyes or seeking guidance from the ceiling can underline this attitude. This kind of communication is not helpful under any circumstance. We all feel this way at times. The ability to turn a negative to a positive is the mark of a mature, thoughtful player. People want to play with the positive player. Apologies are too easy when mistakes are made. The most common statements in volleyball are, Sorry, or, My fault. Occasional, appropriate apologies are okay but are generally meaningless. A commitment to what you are *going to do* is more helpful—I am going to take line and dig lips! Of course, you need to do it, not just talk. Always congratulate good efforts and plays. Offer support when a play is missed. Positive behavior-interpreted communication in tight situations is most important. What does it mean to say, Come on! Let's go! Does it mean we're leaving now? Better yet, use behavior-interpreted communication, such as, Take this guy's angle! or, I've got the setter tip! The voice inflection will indicate the positive, committed attitude.

GAMES AND TACTICS

Doubles

Rules:	Refer to the official guide of the USVBA.
Venues:	Sand, grass, and gym surfaces
More information:	Association of Volleyball Professionals, 100 Corporate Pointe, Suite 100, Culver City, CA 90230.

Beach doubles, particularly the variety played on the golden beaches of Southern California, have spawned the vast majority of the great U.S. volleyball players. The legendary American competitive edge has been honed on the winner's court: If you win, you play; if you don't, sit down; if you don't like it, see ya. On any day you go to play, put your name on a list hanging from one of the court's net poles. Either bring a partner or find one. When it is your turn, you play whoever has won the last game. Beat them and you stay, lose and you put your name on the list and sit. You either are willing to stick with it or find another beach activity. The process develops the tough competitor and discourages the casual player. This tradition has played out on a daily basis for decades.

The Pro Beach Tour was born in this environment. It has created a cult following, developed into a media darling, and is the most visible form of volleyball in the U.S. The prize money increases each year. The professional players train intensely as they prepare for the rigors of each tournament and the length of the tour. The lure of the money and media attention can make players serious, but they still have fun playing.

Doubles volleyball is simple to organize and understand and is fun to play. It can be played under virtually any condition. It can be intensely competitive or a casual social activity. It is a great coed game.

Strategies are relatively simple. The general principle of exposing your strengths and hiding your weaknesses is especially obvious in doubles. The key to successful doubles play is a balance of skills and compatibility between partners.

It is a sure bet that a weak serve receiver will get served if the partner is an outstanding passer (Figure 11.2). If the serve receiving is imbalanced, the only ploy is to have the good passer cover the whole court, which is virtually impossible and very fatiguing.

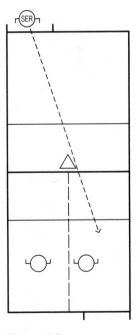

Figure 11.2
Doubles: serve receive

If the opposition's passing is balanced, when you prepare to serve, determine which player you want to set. Then serve the other one. Often one player will be a superior setter. Ideally, you want the weaker setter to set.

Good partners are strong passers and setters. When serving to such a team, determine which player you want hitting. Serve that player long and short. Force a difficult adjustment to approach to hit. Try to fatigue a player. Be aware of the hitter's favorite shot from the left and right so that you can get into the best position to dig. If you or your partner is a better blocker than digger, then consider blocking. Of course, understand that you give up a big area of the court when blocking. Effective blocking requires a tough serve so that the opponent has a difficult time controlling the ball, thereby making sets predictable and allowing the blocker time to position (Figures 11.3 and 11.4). The occasional ambush block can be effective. Pick the right time, show a digging position, then, as the setter is focusing on the set and the hitter is scrambling to approach, quickly come to the net and ambush the hitter. If the gamble pays off and you get a stuff, the memory will cause your opponent to hesitate in future attacks.

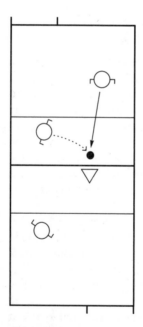

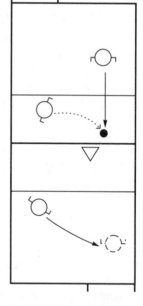

Figure 11.3

Doubles: The blocker takes the line. The digger's position is based on the location of the set, the hitter's range, and the blocker's range. Processing the unfolding conditions as early as possible leads to correct choices.

Figure 11.4

Doubles: The blocker takes the crosscourt. The digger must focus on the hitter's tendencies, the timing of the approach and the height of the set (Does he or she have time to hit the line?), and deciding and adjusting.

If the opponent is attempting to block your partner's attack you must communicate that a blocker is up and what area of the court is open: The blocker is up! Hit line! (or Hit crosscourt!).

There are many individual tactics that unveil themselves as you play. For example, if you read fatigue in one of the opposing players, it is shrewd to make him or her pass, hit, and dig everything. Competitive doubles accentuate the principle of going to the well until it is dry. For example, if a player is struggling at passing, then serve him or her.

Doubles can be a game of who blinks first. It requires consistency over time. When playing doubles, make sure that all participants are on the same page: If it is a social activity, going to the well and poking away at someone's weakness may not be the most diplomatic ploy. Be sensitive to and prepared for the environment in which you choose to compete.

Triples

> Rules: Adapt regular rules
>
> Venues: All

Triples is one of the best ways to train for six-player volleyball. The basic components are present: three contacts-three players, one or two blockers, two hitters. Common digger/blocker relationships can be established. The setter has two options. The hitters can be split, one in front and the other behind, or both can be in front with a quick set or play set in the middle.

Triples is played in a *dynamic triangle*. The triangle adjusts to the situation as it unfolds.

Serve Receive   Receive with two passers (Figure 11.5). The ability of the players to serve receive determines how much court each can cover. One player can pass a big area while another can pass a small area. The third player is near the net ready to set the second contact. If a team is hurting you with a short serve, the player near the net can back off and take it. A team can also receive three across; however, this allows the server to pick his or her target and take out the preferred setter.

Attack   Basically there are two hitters. The primary goal always is to give the hitter a good swing at the ball. The next goal is to force the blocker to have to move as far as possible to perform his or her duties. The most practical tactic is to have one hitter far to the left and the other on the right (Figure 11.5). A quick with a wide secondary set can also be effective but a greater risk. A left-handed setter provides the chance for a strike on second contact, assuming that the setter is positioned facing the left side of the court. Any setter is a threat if he or she is jumping and can dump the ball.

The spikers should try to hit in between the back-row diggers, forcing them to move to retrieve. If all defenders are back, then it's bombs away. Blast the ball. Still try to hit gaps, but apply heat. Tips can be effective if they are intermingled

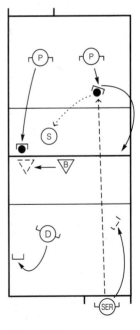

Figure 11.5
Triples: serve receive and subsequent moves

with fire. A tipping, off-speed, junk attack will be gobbled up by a good triples team.

Serving   The general principles of volleyball apply. A short serve can be effective because it forces a potential hitter near the net and disrupts a good approach, thereby forcing the setter to set the other spiker and, thus, making it easier to establish good defensive positions.

Blocking   One blocker is the most common tactical deployment. Occasionally two blockers are used, but a wily hitter will immediately dump the ball into the available open court. Using the two-blocker ambush ploy can be effective on occasion and can turn momentum when discretely applied. One blocker must concentrate on a stable jump and take away one shot, forcing the hitter to hit elsewhere. If a blocker tries to cover the waterfront, leaks will occur everywhere. It is best to choose one shot and take it. The diggers (D in Figures 11.6 and 11.7) can then concentrate on the court areas susceptible to attack.

Digging   The back-row players learn to read the attacker and the options available, and react accordingly (Figure 11.8). They need to know the blocker's intentions. This should be communicated prior to the serve. The blocking strategy is linked to the serve if the goal is to take out one of the hitters. The unfolding of the play will make the final determination of the blocker's position and the diggers' response. Sound, consistent execution of proper defensive technique and principles will pay dividends in digs.

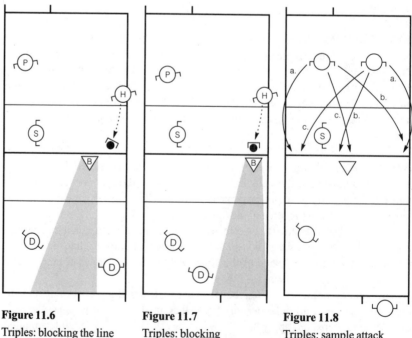

Figure 11.6
Triples: blocking the line

Figure 11.7
Triples: blocking crosscourt

Figure 11.8
Triples: sample attack patterns

Triples is a great *deep-court* game. Specify that all attacks must be made by a hitter taking off from behind the 3-meter line. The emphasis is on ball control and floor defense and results in longer rallies. When playing coed triples on a women's-height net, have the men hit deep court and the women hit anywhere. Many drills preparing a six-player team are organized using triples as a base.

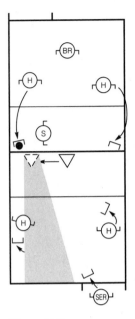

Figure 11.9

Fours: dynamic diamond, one blocker

Fours

Venue: All

Rules: Standard

Doubles and triples tournaments are quite common. Traditionally, fours has only been played whenever eight players were available; however, an outdoor, four-person team tour was recently organized. Fours is a good game to play. There are more tactical responses available than in triples.

Triples is played in triangles. Fours is played in *dynamic diamonds* (Figures 11.9 and 11.10). The *server* is a *back-row player* (BR) who cannot attack at the net. Rotation is normal, so each player is in the back row one out of every four rotations.

Serve Receive   Three passers can now be used while the setter, out of the line of fire, is available for setting duties. However, if only two players are good receivers, hiding the weaker passers should be considered. The weaker passers will be served if available. The setter can be the back-row player, enabling a three-hitter front-row attack. Otherwise, the setter is at the net with two front-row attackers and the potential of a third out of the back row.

Attacking   Team attack patterns can be nearly as complex as in six-player volleyball. However, because the defense consists of only four players, there is really no practical need for a multiple attack. If a team chooses to run a complex system either as an art form or to impress observers, then those objectives justify the inherent risks. There is some value in setting up a back-row attack. If a player is capable of bringing smoke out of the back row, running the two front-row attackers to one side and setting the back-row hitter can be very effective. Fours is a great game to learn the rudiments of the six-player multiple-attack systems.

Serving   The standard tactical principles apply.

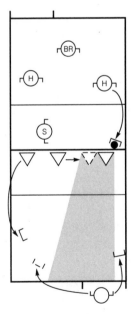

Figure 11.10

Fours: dynamic diamond, two blockers

Blocking   Two-player blocks can be consistently employed. However, if there is only one good blocker and three terrific back-row players, then a one-blocker strategy may be the best option. Basically, the middle-front player and the player on the side of the point of attack form the block. The tactics and related communication are the same as in triples.

Digging   Give up the back court area the block is shadowing. Fours teaches the important back-row responsibilities of the block. If the block is stable in forming, there will be a part of the back row unavailable for an opponent's hard hit. Therefore, the diggers can position accordingly.

Fours is a great way to begin learning the complexities of the six-player game. Specialties will emerge. Setters will set. Blockers will match up more often. Hitters will be placed in positions where they are most effective. The back-row hitters will surface.

Fives?

There is no description of fives. Playing with five players on each side is the most difficult to organize. Nothing seems to fit. Sometimes you are forced to play fives because the number of people requires it. If this happens, suggest playing fours, with a player rotating in and out at the serving position; play triples with three teams; irritate someone so that he or she leaves; or you leave and try to find a reasonable number of people to play. Playing fives is terrible at best. Try it and you will see.

COED VOLLEYBALL

All varieties of volleyball can be played with coed teams. The general principles of play are applicable. There are specific rules that govern six-player coed games and can be found in the official guide of the USVBA.

There can be problems in playing coed volleyball that have more to do with our cultural mores than with tactics and technique. In many parts of the U.S., women have been more exposed to formal training in volleyball than men. Regrettably, few boys and men get a chance to learn and compete in volleyball because of the extremely limited number of middle and high school boys' varsity programs nationwide. If boys do play, it is usually an accident of place of birth. Girls varsity volleyball, on the other hand, is widespread. When Title IX was enacted in the 1970s to ensure equal opportunity for girls and women in competitive sports and other extracurricular activities in federally funded institutions, volleyball was established as one of the formal activities. Its popularity and quality of play has exploded.

Unfortunately, as a result of Title IX, many schools are eliminating boys' sports rather than increasing girls' sports as a way of meeting gender-equity issues. Instead of adding to the variety of sports in which girls can participate, Title IX, in effect, has reduced athletic opportunities for both boys and girls. Sadly, many boys interested in competitive volleyball specifically have no legislation to ensure a variety of athletic opportunities and, therefore, must participate in the limited, traditional offerings. In addition, both boys and girls have very little chance of participating in other Olympic sports such as rowing, cycling, and so on.

So, when players of both genders gather to play a little volleyball, there can be some confusion as to who has the skills and who traditionally dominates competitive sports. If the participants can put aside the cultural and social elements and focus on exposing strengths and hiding weaknesses, coed volleyball is a superb activity in any variety.

The Six-Player Game

12

Even though there are many people who prefer the games of volleyball requiring fewer players, six-player volleyball is the entree; the other games are the appetizers. They are prepared with fewer ingredients. Sixes is the consummate gourmet dish. The basic skills are a must. But the opportunities for strategies and tactics, adjustments, and the coordination of human resources are unsurpassed. Being a part of a team that can smoothly execute with discipline in the world's most reactive and spontaneous game brings immense satisfaction. Being a part of a unit of individuals that can blend a variety of talent through cooperation and communication makes six-player volleyball very special. The taste is exquisite.

PLAYING SYSTEMS

The organization of the six-player game requires the blending of five systems: team serve receive, side-out attack, blocking, back-row defense, and transition attack. These systems demand attention as separate entities, even though they look like a swirl of continuous action to the casual observer.

Traditionally, teams describe their general *system of play* through a rotational order that refers to the offense. Combinations of numbers are used to describe how many players have hitting and/or setting duties. The first number represents how many players have hitting responsibility. The second number refers to the number of setters. Therefore, a 5-1 offensive system has five spikers and one setter; a 4-2 has four spikers and two setters; a 6-2 has six spikers, two of which also are setters in specific situations; and a 6-6 is the simplest system, in which each player sets when he or she is in the middle-front position.

The basic offensive systems include the 4-2, 6-2, and 5-1. There are other modifications that are either very simple and are used at social outings (such as the 6-6), or there are adaptations of the basics to take advantage of specific athletic abilities (such as the unbalanced 5-1). A 3-3 system is so old it might become new.

The following descriptions will cover the offensive components of the 4-2, 6-2, and 5-1. The serve-receive patterns, blocking, and floor defensive systems covered can be adapted to any of the offensive systems. Further, specific team attack tactics can be employed within each system. For example, the *swing offense*—a multilayered attack scheme—the *31X spread,* and the basic *X* series can be used within each design. These tactics will be generally referred to but not described in this book. They are mentioned to give you a general understanding of the potential complexities of volleyball and to bait you into further study.

There are several variations to these basic systems that attempt to take advantage of a team's players' strengths as well as to exploit the opponent's weaknesses. Most likely the best and most effective variations have yet to be discovered.

This chapter contains many court diagrams in which player positions are identified by capital letters. Following is a list of the abbreviations used and the positions they represent:

LS	Left-side hitter	Q_2	Multiple quick hitter
RS	Right-side hitter	OP	Opposite
S	Setter	LF	Left front
WS	Weak-side attacker	LB	Left back
QH	Quick hitter	RF	Right front
OH_1	Primary left-side hitter	RB	Right back
OH_2	Primary right-side hitter	MF	Middle front
Q_1	Adjacent quick hitter	MB	Middle back

It is also important to note that all underscored positions in the diagrams represent front-row players.

The Basic 4-2 System

The 4-2 is the most elementary of the competitive offensive systems. (If people have never played or are just getting together for a social game, the most elementary system would be the 6-6, in which everyone sets when they rotate to middle front and hits when they are on either frontcourt side.) Originally, the 4-2 was developed to accommodate good ball handlers who were often short and quick and who specialized in delivering high, outside sets to big, slavering attackers who could bring the heat.

In the early days, the rules prohibited blockers from reaching over the net, so complex attack routes and quick sets and play sets were not needed to deceive the block. When the blockers were given the green light to reach over to stuff the ball, offenses were forced to become more creative and deceptive. Likewise, the setter's ability to block became important, putting pressure on short setters. Blockers began to shut down the standard, outside high-ball attack. It became evident that offenses needed to utilize the maximum number of attackers allowed. The short, front-row setter became a white elephant.

The 4-2 is presently seeing a renaissance, however. With the advent of the back-row attack, big waterbug-quick setters who jump set, hit, or dump left-handed, and creative serve-receive patterns that allow greater hitter movement, the old 4-2 with a new sheen is back.

4-2 Advantages

- Pinpoint serve receive is not required.
- Minimal movement is required of the setter to get to the target.
- The attacker's routes are less complex than in other systems.
- Attackers get lots of work and develop a good hitting rhythm.

4-2 Disadvantages

- There can be limited offensive options.
- Having two different setters means having two different dispositions, styles, timings, and tactical approaches to which attackers must adjust.
- The setter must divide his or her attention between setting duties and the serve receive and other back-row tasks.
- There is limited ability to adjust to the opponent.
- The transition game is limited.
- Hitters can get overworked or shut down by the opponent's defenses.

4-2 Personnel Requirements

- Two setters of comparable ability who can also receive serve.
- Two key attackers who can hit against a static, big block: The *left-side attacker* is the primary attacker who hits from the left side and in front of the setter (also known as ace attackers, cannons, onside hitters, power hitters, on-hand hitters). The *right-side attacker* is the secondary attacker who hits primarily from the right side—unless left-handed—and mainly from behind the setter (also known as offside, or weak-side, hitters).
- Two attackers who have good all-around ability and can take pressure off the key hitters.

4-2 Basic Tactics (Figure 12.1)

- Set up the team with the left-side attackers lining up in serve receive so that they hit left twice and right once. (In rotational order, the left-side hitter precedes the setter.)
- Setters will be working most of the time with certain hitters, therefore, match up setters most compatible with the hitters on either side of them in the rotation.
- Start the strongest attackers left front.
- Start the best setter (if compatible with the best hitter) left back.
- Start a left-handed attacker.
- The setter, when setting, should always face the left side for easier delivery.

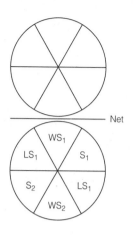

Net

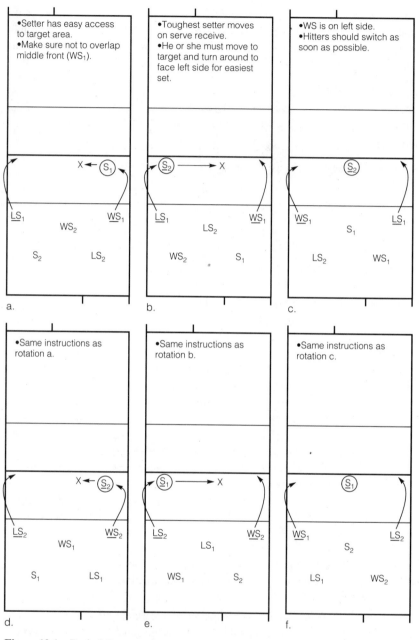

a.
•Setter has easy access to target area.
•Make sure not to overlap middle front (WS_1).

b.
•Toughest setter moves on serve receive.
•He or she must move to target and turn around to face left side for easiest set.

c.
•WS is on left side.
•Hitters should switch as soon as possible.

d.
•Same instructions as rotation a.

e.
•Same instructions as rotation b.

f.
•Same instructions as rotation c.

Figure 12.1 Basic 4-2 system

The Basic 6-2 System

The 6-2 is similar to the 4-2 only in that it employs two setters opposite each other in the rotational order. The major difference is that instead of the active setter being the one in the front row, the *setter in the back row* carries out the setting chores. As this system developed to counter bigger, more sophisticated blocking schemes, considerably more attack patterns were employed. But there were some problems getting the back-row setter into the target area.

A common modification used during the 1960s (and occasionally today) was to use two *technique players*. They lined up in the rotation immediately preceding the setters. They each set one rotation when the setter was left back. The theory behind this ploy is that it is easier for the right-back player to get to the target. The left-back player has to travel a much longer distance, weave through other players, and turn around to face the left side. The trade-off is that four different players deliver the sets and, thus, there is little continuity.

6-2 Advantages

- Three front-row attackers allow for greater offensive options.
- Attackers can specialize: Quick hitters hit quicks; play-set hitters run the second option; release hitters hit release.
- Players seem more enthusiastic about the increased flexibility of the more complex system.
- There are increased tactical options to adjust to different teams.
- Players' special strengths and specializations can be utilized.
- If a team has only two good or experienced players, they can be in the setting positions and, if need be, virtually play doubles (because the front-row setter can pass and hit while the back-row setter sets).

6-2 Disadvantages

- A breakdown in required serve-receive accuracy leads to offensive-pattern confusion.
- The system revolves around the quick attack. If, because of poor serve receive, the quick hitter cannot get available to attack or the player is not skilled enough to hit effectively, then the 6-2-designed advantage of multiple options is reduced to a difficult one- or two-option offense.
- Because the attackers focus on running patterns, they often do not concentrate enough on serve receive and are not nearly as accurate as this precise system requires.
- Because they have to move from the back row, the setters often do not get to target and wind up in poor body position to accurately set the ball.
- Having two setters means having two different styles.
- Oftentimes, very good potential attackers are quick hitters. Because a quick attacker requires a good pass, these hitters get little work and are wasted.
- Hours of practice are required to perfect the system.

6-2 System Elements

- The serve receive is good.
- The setter runs efficient routes to target and gets into position.
- All attackers make themselves available and time their approaches according to the called-play pattern.

- The setter delivers accurate sets and makes the correct set selection.
- The attacker hits smart shots.

If these elements are functioning, the system is virtually unstoppable. However, if the system breaks down, particularly the serve receive, which usually precipitates all other malfunctions, then the 6-2 becomes grist for the defense's scoring mill.

An important footnote is required here: It is possible that both combatants are using the 6-2 or another high-risk system, so the breakdowns may cancel each other out.

6-2 Personnel Requirements

Setters. Two relatively evenly matched players of comparable ability are needed to set the ball with accuracy and intelligence. They also need to be able to attack effectively and have a good standing reach and/or ability to jump well.

Quick attackers. Two players who should be tall, with a high reach. They must be able to adjust to the setter's position and make themselves available to get a good swing at the ball. They must be able to move the ball around the blockers. They must be able to get off the net in transition and get up to threaten the middle legitimately, *every time.* Most likely, they will be middle blockers. Therefore, they must possess blocking skills. They must be good jumpers with exceptional endurance.

Outside hitters. (Depending on the front-row setter's hitting responsibilities, these two outside hitters could be play-set/right-side hitters or left-side/release hitters.) They must be mobile, quick, and always get a good approach. They should be "rhythm hitters"—hitters who get into a good approach and hitting rhythm and always get a good swing at the ball. They must be able to block outside, set the block, and either cut off the lines or funnel the attack into the middle blocker. They must be able to receive serve with precise accuracy.

Skill Requirements to Effectively Run a 6-2

- Your setters and quick hitters should be able to connect (that is, the setter delivers accurate sets, and the quick hitters attack the ball with control and force) *eight to nine out of ten* off a perfect toss.
- With your team in a full serve-receive pattern (in each of the six rotations), the quick attack should be available with control and fire power *five to six out of ten* for high school teams, *six to seven times out of ten* for college teams, and *seven to nine times out of ten* for national teams.
- Likewise, the play set should be available based on the same formula. (Based on the above numbers, a coach should consider tactical, personnel, or technical changes if a team is unable to execute off a serve against no defense.)
- The setter should be in the target area in the correct body posture from any rotational position *before the serve is touched* by a serve receiver. (It

takes a serve from 2 to 4 seconds to go from server to receiver.) The setter should be able to get to target from the right back or middle back in under 1.1 seconds. From the left back, the setter should make the trip in under 1.3 seconds, leaving plenty of time to get into good position. The chase after any errant pass should be initiated *from the target area,* not en route. Not getting into good setting position is due totally to a setter's laziness and a coach's lack of attention to detail.

- During a game, how many points does your team give up as a direct result of the system's breakdown (unforced errors)? If you are giving up five or more points, that's a third of the game! You should consider simplifying your playing system.

- When analyzing statistics after a match and/or season, determine which hitters are getting the most work and who is the most effective. If your quick hitters are getting *less than 25 percent* of the total swings, then a modification of the system should be considered.

6-2 Basic Tactics (Figure 12.2)

- The best serve receivers should be passing the biggest areas.
- Quick hitters must always be available relative to a setter's position.

The Quick Hitter-Setter Relationship

The setter must

- Get to the ball
- Establish approximately a 45-degree angle with the net, with the feet and shoulders facing the left side
- Set the ball from above his or her head
- Set the ball high enough with appropriate speed for the hitter
- Cover

The quick hitter must

- Adjust his or her starting position to the setter's position
- Approach so that, when in the air, he or she is behind an imaginary extended line from the setter to the net
- Raise his or her hitting arm high to give the setter a target
- Be consistent in timing the jump
- Communicate where he or she is

The Basic 5-1 System

At the 1968 Olympics in Mexico City, the All Japan Men's Team popularized the 5-1 system around their legendary setter Katatushi Nekota. They developed the system in the mid-1960s. Mexico City showcased what was to become the most commonly used system in the world at all levels.

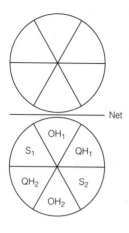

Net

Note: setters could be outside hitters here; however, to simplify the chart, setters are in the left-side hitting position (also known as **release hitting**).

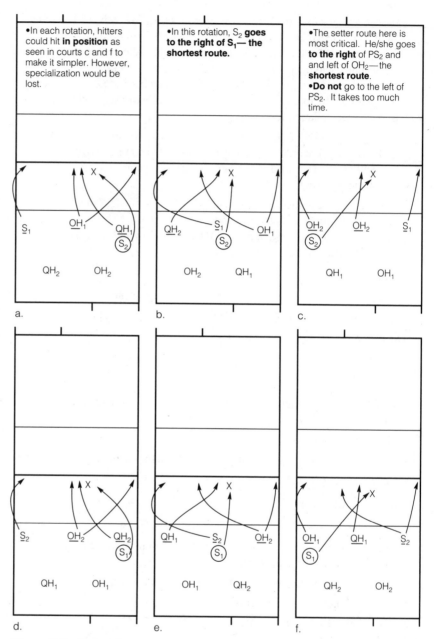

•In each rotation, hitters could hit **in position** as seen in courts c and f to make it simpler. However, specialization would be lost.

•In this rotation, S_2 **goes to the right of S_1— the shortest route.**

•The setter route here is most critical. He/she goes **to the right** of PS_2 and and left of OH_2—the **shortest route**.
•**Do not** go to the left of PS_2. It takes too much time.

a. b. c.

d. e. f.

Figure 12.2 Basic 6-2 system

This system is a combination of the 4-2 and 6-2. It is simple, yet it can be flexible and complex. It optimizes players' strengths and simplifies tasks for most.

The 5-1 system is *setter centered,* that is, it is built around the ability of the setter. He or she is the sole leader of the offense and can concentrate on this very important task. Each attacker's relationship to the setter is unique because of the setter's exclusive position based on rotational order. Tactics can be specific by rotation. Attack patterns are designed for each rotation (Figure 12.3).

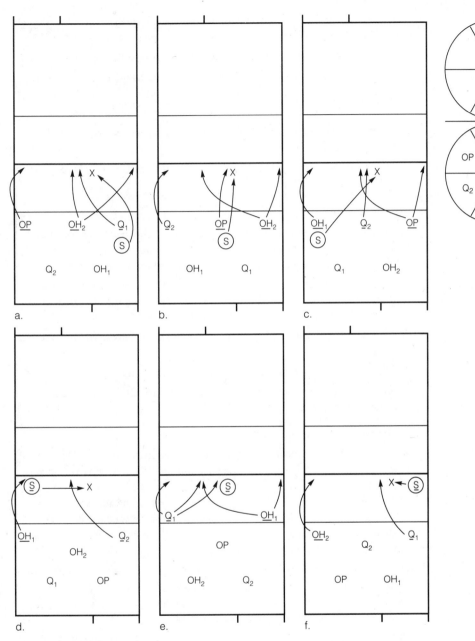

Figure 12.3 Basic 5-1 system

5-1 Advantages

- One setter means technical and tactical continuity.
- The setter can concentrate on one main task.
- The best athlete can function best in the setting position because, usually, he or she will be involved in every three-contact series.

- The setter can singularly affect winning or losing more than any other player because of his or her strong role and ball contact on virtually every series.
- Players' roles are more specialized and carry less general responsibilities.
- There is less pressure on the serve receive than in the 6-2 (but more than in the 4-2).
- Tactical matchups are more flexible due to the different rotation looks.
- In practice, the setter does not have to divide time between setting and hitting.
- Due to specialized playing roles, the coach-player relationship is very clear and it's easy to train the team.

5-1 Disadvantages

- There is tremendous pressure on the setter. This athlete must be technically and tactically sound and consistent and must temper these skills with strong leadership. The role requires a very strong, competent, steady individual.
- It is difficult to substitute in the setting position. If the starting setter is injured, a cold, inexperienced player usually replaces the starter, changing the rhythm, continuity, and confidence level.
- If the serve receive goes bad, the team can get bogged down when the setter is in the front row.
- If the setter has a bad match, often the team follows suit.
- Because the players specialize, they may have difficulty responding to needed tactical adjustments.

5-1 Personnel Requirements

Setter(s). This person must be strong and balanced in three areas: (1) technical execution, (2) tactical knowledge and play and set selection, and (3) leadership, or being able to get the most out of the hitters. The setter must know what psychological buttons to push to get results out of the attackers. Being tall and left-handed could be an advantage so that at the net the setter is also an attacking threat on the second contact. The setter must be able to jump set.

Adjacent quick hitter (Q_1). This player must be a strong individual hitter who has many shots, must have the ability to hit a variety of sets, must be able to block well (often, if the setter is small, the adjacent quick hitter will have to help the setter with blocking), and must have endurance to approach the middle quick attack through an entire five-game match.

Multiple quick hitter (Q_2). This player must meet the same requirements as the 6-2 quick hitter.

Release hitter (OH_1). This person must be able to hit effectively against a multiple block, must have endurance to carry a heavy attack load through a long match, must be an effective left-side hitter but capable of hitting on the right side, and must be a good serve receiver.

Opposite (OP). This player must be the most versatile hitter and must be able to hit all three positions (or at least convince the opponent that this is a likelihood). This hitter has decoy responsibilities and must be convincing. This player is the auxiliary setter, being opposite the setter in the rotation, and must be able to at least set well to the outside. He or she must be a good serve receiver. This is probably the best all-around player after the setter.

Play-set hitter (OH$_2$). This player is primarily a right-side hitter and must be quick and be able to hit to the right and left of the quick hitter. This player must be able to run the prescribed routes behind the quick hitter and adjust to the pass and setter position and always get available. He or she must be a good serve receiver.

The setter should be surrounded by the two best individual hitters because they are up at the net twice with only one other attacker.

SERVE-RECEIVE PATTERNS/SYSTEMS

Just as the setter is the key individual player to a successful offense, so a successful serve receive is the key team goal to running a smooth offensive system. Without a consistent serve receive, there is no chance of taking what looks good on paper and putting it on the floor. The actual offensive system is only as good as the serve receive.

Serve-Receive Pattern Principles

- Expose the best serve receivers.
- Good serve receivers prefer to be unencumbered in big areas of responsibility. They are not hemmed in. They are aggressive passers who need room to pursue the ball.
- An average passer or player whose priority is to get into an attack mode quickly should have a small area to pass.
- The serve-receive pattern should have the setter in a position to get into the target easily and quickly.
- If possible, the attacker should be in an optimal starting position to affect the offensive system.

Figures 12.4 through 12.8 show positions and describe advantages and disadvantages. **Note:** When creating a serve-receive pattern, keep the overlap rule in mind: A player cannot overlap adjacent teammates prior to serve contact. The serve-receive patterns shown may be used by the same team in the same game and vary by rotation. They are shown here through all rotations based on the positions of the setter. The international rotation grid is included in Figures 12.4 through 12.6. The pattern descriptions occasionally refer to specific, numbered rotation positions, and these grids are illustrated here for your reference.

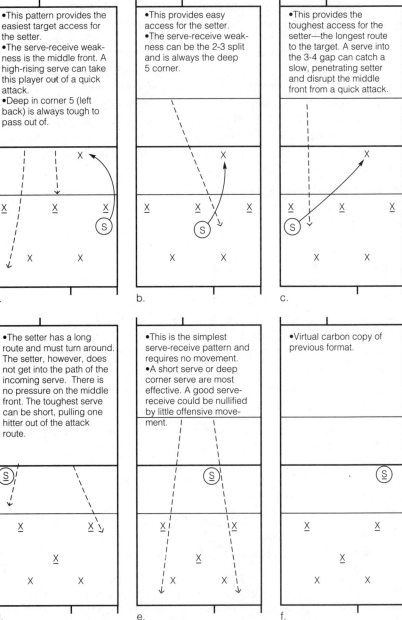

| 4 | 3 | 2 |
| 5 | 6 | 1 |

International Rotation Grid

a.
•This pattern provides the easiest target access for the setter.
•The serve-receive weakness is the middle front. A high-rising serve can take this player out of a quick attack.
•Deep in corner 5 (left back) is always tough to pass out of.

b.
•This provides easy access for the setter.
•The serve-receive weakness can be the 2-3 split and is always the deep 5 corner.

c.
•This provides the toughest access for the setter—the longest route to the target. A serve into the 3-4 gap can catch a slow, penetrating setter and disrupt the middle front from a quick attack.

d.
•The setter has a long route and must turn around. The setter, however, does not get into the path of the incoming serve. There is no pressure on the middle front. The toughest serve can be short, pulling one hitter out of the attack route.

e.
•This is the simplest serve-receive pattern and requires no movement.
•A short serve or deep corner serve are most effective. A good serve-receive could be nullified by little offensive movement.

f.
•Virtual carbon copy of previous format.

Figure 12.4 Five-player serve receive, showing different setter penetration positions: *Advantage.* Passers cover the entire court; this is a good pattern for an inexperienced, immobile, average-passing team. *Disadvantage.* It exposes too many serving targets.

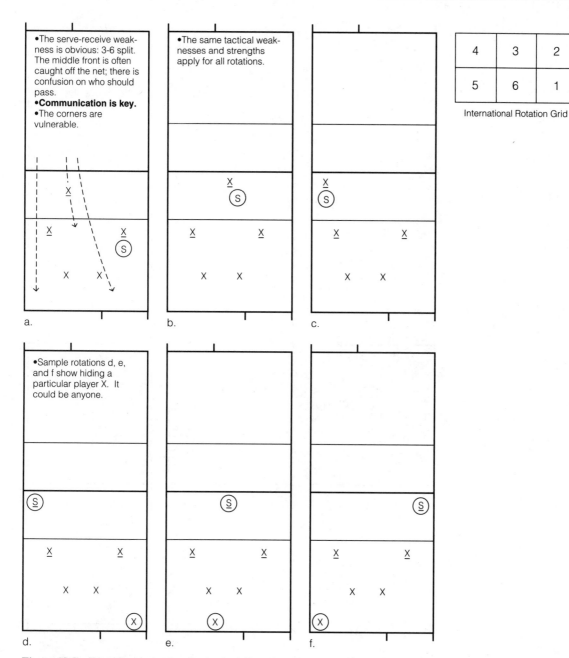

- The serve-receive weakness is obvious: 3-6 split. The middle front is often caught off the net; there is confusion on who should pass.
- **Communication is key.**
- The corners are vulnerable.

a.

- The same tactical weaknesses and strengths apply for all rotations.

b.

c.

4	3	2
5	6	1

International Rotation Grid

- Sample rotations d, e, and f show hiding a particular player X. It could be anyone.

d.

e.

f.

Figure 12.5   Four-player serve receive (or "cup"): *Advantages*. The setter can get closer to the target. This pattern can hide a player (usually a hitter) for better attack access and can expose better receivers. *Disadvantage*. Big areas are vulnerable to tough serves, forcing a lot of movement during the serve receive.

4	3	2
5	6	1

International Rotation Grid

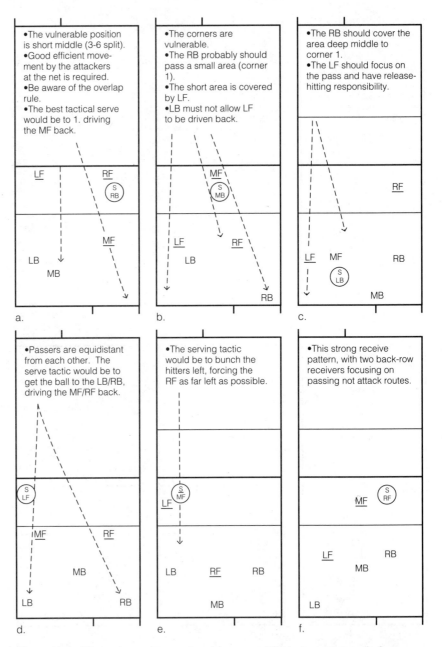

a.

- The vulnerable position is short middle (3-6 split).
- Good efficient movement by the attackers at the net is required.
- Be aware of the overlap rule.
- The best tactical serve would be to 1. driving the MF back.

b.

- The corners are vulnerable.
- The RB probably should pass a small area (corner 1).
- The short area is covered by LF.
- LB must not allow LF to be driven back.

c.

- The RB should cover the area deep middle to corner 1.
- The LF should focus on the pass and have release-hitting responsibility.

d.

- Passers are equidistant from each other. The serve tactic would be to get the ball to the LB/RB, driving the MF/RF back.

e.

- The serving tactic would be to bunch the hitters left, forcing the RF as far left as possible.

f.

- This strong receive pattern, with two back-row receivers focusing on passing not attack routes.

Figure 12.6 Three-player serve receive: *Advantages*. This pattern exposes the best receivers and gives them a tremendous range to roam. Serve receive roles are clear-cut. *Disadvantages*. The serve can be hit into big areas, which makes this pattern vulnerable to power serves. Aggressive receivers will collide as a result of poor communication. Receiver must cover a considerable distance, and the serve receive often ends with an ace. **Note:** These rotations are showing player positions consistent with strong and weak passers.

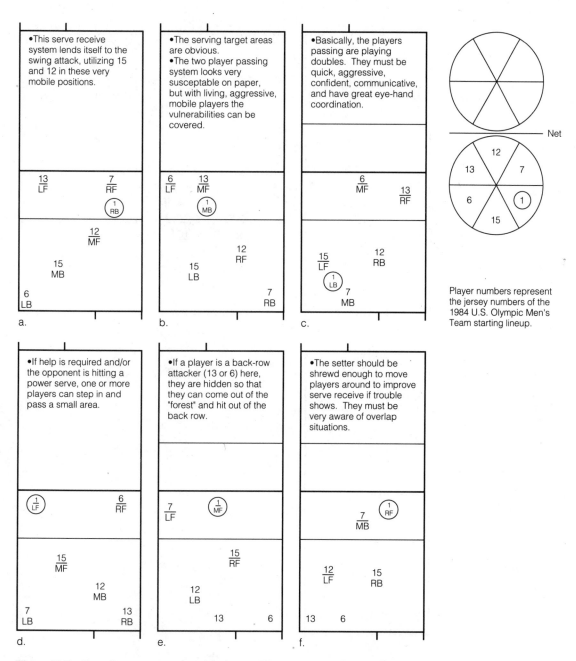

a.
- This serve receive system lends itself to the swing attack, utilizing 15 and 12 in these very mobile positions.

13 LF		7 RF
		(1 RB)
	12 MF	
15 MB		
6 LB		

b.
- The serving target areas are obvious.
- The two player passing system looks very susceptible on paper, but with living, aggressive, mobile players the vulnerabilities can be covered.

6 LF	13 MF	
	(1 MB)	
		12 RF
15 LB		
		7 RB

c.
- Basically, the players passing are playing doubles. They must be quick, aggressive, confident, communicative, and have great eye-hand coordination.

6 MF	13 RF
15 LF	
(1 LB)	12 RB
7 MB	

Player numbers represent the jersey numbers of the 1984 U.S. Olympic Men's Team starting lineup.

d.
- If help is required and/or the opponent is hitting a power serve, one or more players can step in and pass a small area.

(1 LF)	6 RF
15 MF	
	12 MB
7 LB	13 RB

e.
- If a player is a back-row attacker (13 or 6) here, they are hidden so that they can come out of the "forest" and hit out of the back row.

7 LF	(1 MF)
	15 RF
12 LB	
13	6

f.
- The setter should be shrewd enough to move players around to improve serve receive if trouble shows. They must be very aware of overlap situations.

7 MB	(1 RF)
12 LF	15 RB
13	6

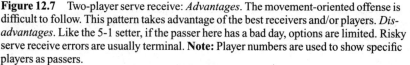

Figure 12.7   Two-player serve receive: *Advantages*. The movement-oriented offense is difficult to follow. This pattern takes advantage of the best receivers and/or players. *Disadvantages*. Like the 5-1 setter, if the passer here has a bad day, options are limited. Risky serve receive errors are usually terminal. **Note:** Player numbers are used to show specific players as passers.

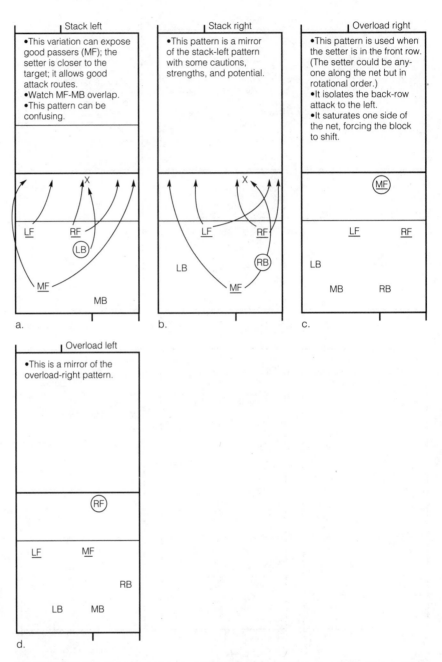

a.

b.

c.

d.

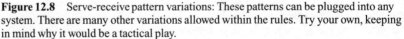

Figure 12.8 Serve-receive pattern variations: These patterns can be plugged into any system. There are many other variations allowed within the rules. Try your own, keeping in mind why it would be a tactical play.

In the serve-receive patterns, it is possible to appear to be in one pattern while actually being in another. For example, a five-player receiving pattern may actually be a two-player receive. It is difficult for the server to see the actual depth or interest a player has in passing. Just by slightly moving the front-row receivers closer to the net (in front of the 3-meter line instead of behind it), you give the two back-row receivers more range to pass.

The setter must be thoroughly knowledgeable of various patterns and overlap rules to be able to make necessary changes to improve passing or attack routes. Two cheap points off a poor serve receive or stagnant attack approaches should prompt the setter to make on-the-court shifts to save time-outs for real disasters.

EFFECTIVE OFFENSIVE-SYSTEM COMMUNICATION

Developing a good communication plan is critical to any system so that players can quickly exchange clear messages, whether playing in a quiet gym or in front of thousands of slavering partisan fans generating enough noise to obliterate even the most conscious thought. Further, the coaching staff must be able to talk to the players utilizing consistent, understandable words, numbers, and symbols.

In the United States, there is a need for a common, descriptive communication for offensive options. This is important for clinics, manuals, books, and a general exchange of knowledge. Coaches need to speak the same language. However, each team can use its own inside system but still understand the common language.

Common Play-Calling Systems

Numbered Set Patterns Some teams have numbers designating specific plays describing the attack route in total. The system is similar to basketball plays. For example, the setter calls "play 1" either verbally or by raising one finger. Play 1 may mean that the left front hits a high, outside set, the middle front hits a quick set next to the setter, and the right front hits a low-back set. The advantages of a single-number set-route system is simplicity and the minimal thinking required of an attacker. The disadvantage is the inability to adjust to a bad pass or to a block that has altered this position.

Numbered Attack Routes and Set Heights There are two ways these can be called: (1) the setter communicates to each hitter what route or set he or she will run either verbally or by hand; (2) prior to the serve, the attackers indicate to the setter what route or set they want. The advantage is flexibility within the plays so that players can adjust to the defense. Among the disadvantages, the hitters may not always get the message, or, if the attackers are calling the route, a hitter may run into another hitter running the same route. There is confusion in independent thought.

Audible System   Each attacker calls his or her route *after* the serve. The call is based on defensive alignments. The advantage is the tremendous flexibility to adjust tactically. The disadvantages are that there can be tremendous confusion and that the setter may not get the message.

Obviously, a combination of the three systems would stabilize the communication process. There are three basic communication methods: numbers (verbal), hand signals, and slang description. A variety of number play-calling systems have been concocted. The one that seems the most logical, is easily understood, and can be used wherever volleyball enthusiasts meet was devised several years ago by Jim Coleman (coach of the 1968 U.S. Men's Olympic Team and one of the best volleyball minds in the world). It has been used by the U.S. men's national team for many years and describes many options (Figure 12.9).

The net is divided into nine zones, each 1 meter wide (see Figure 12.19a). The zones are numbered 1 to 9 from left to right as the player faces the net. Sets are numbered according to the height and speed of delivery. The lower the number, the quicker the set and lower the set trajectory. A quick set, then, would be a 1. Usually a high set would be a 10, even though numbers higher than 5 are seldom used.

When a set is described, two numbers are used. The first number indicates the zone in which the ball is set. The second number describes the height and speed of delivery. Therefore, a 14 would be a set approximately 4 feet at its apex above the net, set out to and attacked in the number 1 zone (Figure 12.9b).

Because the back-row attack is an integral part of many offenses, we now describe the areas from where the back-row hitters ply their trade. The back row is divided into four equal corridors perpendicular to the 3-meter line and the net. Chris Marlowe, captain of the 1984 U.S. Men's Olympic Team, coined the term "pipe" for the exact middle of the court, between corridors C and B. It is duly recorded and accepted (Figure 12.9c).

The numbering and lettering system is a mouthful. If a setter were attempting to verbalize each option to the front-row hitters and two back-row attackers, several points and minutes could pass before the tactical utterance could be completed. Therefore, the system is used in skull sessions, scouting reports, clinics, barroom arguments, descriptions of exact placements, and any other confrontations during which time is no object but precise description is.

Game situations and quick message-sending dictate that you abbreviate the system. Hand signals are best to overcome deafening crowd noise or to keep the next play from an opponent who speaks the same language.

There is little need for a universal hand-signal system. However, each team needs to have some nonverbal communication to call plays. It can be showing fingers or hand positions to indicate patterns. Another option is touching a part of the uniform. The beauty of being able to call plays with one hand is that it is easily concealed from the opponent. Touching parts of the uniform may require several

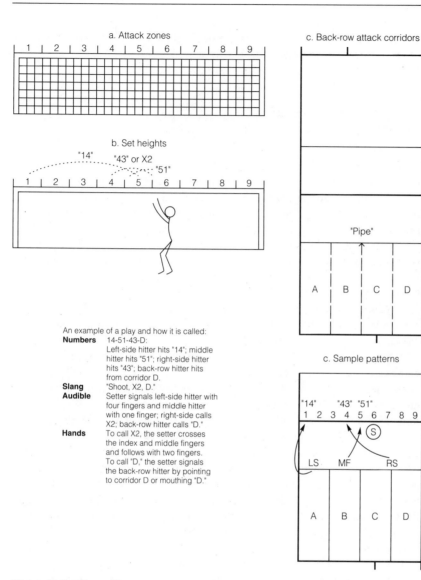

a. Attack zones

b. Set heights

"14" "43" or X2 "51"

c. Back-row attack corridors

"Pipe"

| A | B | C | D |

An example of a play and how it is called:

Numbers   14-51-43-D:
Left-side hitter hits "14"; middle hitter hits "51"; right-side hitter hits "43"; back-row hitter hits from corridor D.

Slang   "Shoot, X2, D."

Audible   Setter signals left-side hitter with four fingers and middle hitter with one finger; right-side calls X2; back-row hitter calls "D."

Hands   To call X2, the setter crosses the index and middle fingers and follows with two fingers. To call "D," the setter signals the back-row hitter by pointing to corridor D or mouthing "D."

c. Sample patterns

"14" "43" "51"

LS   MF   RS

| A | B | C | D |

Figure 12.9   Play calling

moves, not unlike a third-base coach flashing signals to the batter. Attackers must get into the habit of looking to the setter for a signal. Several teams reverse this process. The attacker will signal the setter what he or she wants to hit. However, this process takes the formulation of the offense out of the setter's hands.

As players play, they will evolve certain slang terms for plays or sets: rip, shoot, quick, flare, X, slide, pipe, hut, pump, and so on. These terms are one-syllable, easily heard, descriptive words. The numbers can be added for further information. Slang terms are also easy to remember. Players can be creative and invested in the development of terms.

Most teams will use a combination of the three communication systems to satisfy the needs of any situation that may arise.

SUPPORT FOR OFFENSIVE SYSTEMS: COVERAGE BEHIND THE ATTACK

Specific coverage responsibilities have diminished as offensive systems have become more complex, involving more players running attack routes with intended deception or at such a speed that they are jumping. A few years ago, this author did a survey of the top international coaches in the world, asking them to list a priority order of the most important (to least important) functions of volleyball. Every coach queried listed attack coverage as the least important. The top priority listed was involving as many players as possible in the movement of the attack.

Certainly, addressing the possibility of every attacker being blocked is important and, of course, can yield the possibility of mounting another attack in the same volley. However, at levels of play where attacking is still relatively simple and individual, the opportunity for the block to form is greater and, therefore, the need to cover the hitter is also greater.

There are basically two situations. The first is covering an individual attacker who obviously is getting the set. This occurs in a system with virtually no quick or play-set attack or when the passing is so poor that everyone in the arena knows the ball is going outside. Here, each player, other than the hitter, has coverage responsibility. It is clear where they should be. The player must always get there and assume the correct position.

Figure 12.10 shows the coverage for a left-front attack. The middle back, left back, and middle front form a cup within 2 meters of the hitter and assume low postures with arms out. The right back is referred to as the swing player and swings into the middle-back position and is responsible for all deep blocks. The right front drops back to the 3-meter line. This formation is the opposite of a right-front attack. The left back becomes the swing player and the right back comes underneath the hitter.

It is simple and should be routine. The demise of this routine is when players get lazy. It must be reinforced in the drills all of the time. The overriding principle is: *Follow the hitter and stay low.*

The second situation is covering a multioption attack. The assumption here is that the setter is coming out of the back row. The emphasis of the combination attack is putting as much pressure on the block through a movement-oriented offense. With more players possibly being set, however, they have less time to focus on coverage. Therefore, the principle here is: *If you don't get the set, cover where you are.*

Because the attackers and setter will be in the general area, coverage can still reap saves. However, it is more difficult because there is less time to get into good body position. (The sets are quicker, and players are jumping and crossing each other's paths.) The two remaining back-row players, if not involved in a back-row attack, must follow the patterns based on the middle quick and then adjust.

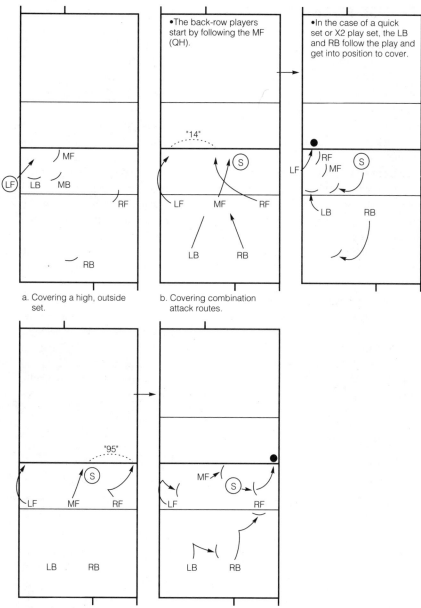

a. Covering a high, outside set.

b. Covering combination attack routes.

c. Covering a back set.

Figure 12.10   Attack coverage

Quick sets and flat-outside sets are more often blocked down inside the 3-meter line than deep. Therefore, the biggest part of the court to be left open is deep (see Figure 12.10). One other note: when the setter and quick hitter are bunched in the middle, they must find an opening and cover the space, avoiding screening each other from the hitter.

DEFENSE FORMATS

As described earlier, rotational orders and playing systems are defined by their offensive application. All defensive schemes can be modified and adjusted to any playing system. It is *defense* that scores most of the points in volleyball. Serving either yields direct points from aces or forces a bad pass, reducing the opponent's attack options and allowing the defense to form on the obvious play. Blockers either stuff a ball for a point or force the attack to make an error (resulting in a point). Also, the block can control the attack so that the back-row defenders can pass the ball for a transition counterstrike.

There are only four ways to score, and all are related to defense except a service ace. However, several relatively illogical elements are commonly used around the world because of the traditional offensive mind-set. Tradition dictates that playing systems be built around offense. For example, setters are often the shortest and least effective blockers on a team, yet they block on the right side, usually facing the opponent's biggest, toughest hitter. The reason is that the offense is usually initiated from right of center. Left-side hitters, often the best blockers, block the left side against the hitter who statistically receives the least number of sets. They block there so they can hit left-side.

The backcourt arrangements are also convened to benefit the offense. The setter, often the best digger, plays right back because it is the shortest distance from the setting position. The right back receives the fewest attacks, while the left back—occupied by one of the bigger, slower defenders—gets the most. The question is, If defense provides either direct points or opportunities to score, then why not position players according to their defensive strengths first and offensive strengths second?

Team Defense Principles

- Put your best blockers on the spiker most likely to hit in any given situation.
- Put your best back-row defenders in areas most likely to be attacked.
- Play back-row defense on help: Stay wide, forcing the opponent to attack in front of the diggers.
- The blockers have back-row responsibility. (They screen an area in the backcourt that cannot be hit hard, allowing the diggers to play in areas around the *block shadow* (Figure 12.11).)

Transition Considerations

Once a ball is controlled, a team must have some way to counterattack. Without solid defense, these opportunities are few.

Transition attack does not need to be elaborate. The opponents are busy getting into their defense and, therefore, cannot form up as easy as in a serve-receive situation. The goal of a transition attack is for the hitter to *get a good swing at the ball*. If the setter cannot get to the ball, then whoever is on the right side sets that play. A simple high ball is needed, with the hitters making themselves available.

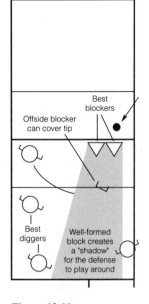

Figure 12.11
Block shadow

There are times that a team can run a full combination attack in transition, but this is secondary to controlling the ball so that a hitter can swing for a point.

Defensive Schemes

Basic blocking tactics are described in Chapter 8. The following schemes can accommodate most blocking tactics. The three most common designs, called out during play, are designated by the colors of the American flag and came out of the National Team Program.

Middle Back Deep (White—Figure 12.12)
This is the most common defensive design. Players can be put into their strongest positions. The line, or "wing," diggers put their outside feet on the line so that if a ball is hit down the line, they only need to dig forward and into the court. If a line digger plays inside the line, then he or she must defend to either side of his or her body.

The crosscourt diggers point their feet crosscourt and twist toward the attack. They line up so that the ball can be seen hit inside the middle blocker. Offside blockers are responsible for anything crosscourt inside the 3-meter line. They must be careful not to cut in front of the crosscourt diggers. Middle back is the most mobile, versatile digger, who can read and react to the intentions of the attack. He or she stays deep within a meter of the back line and generally lines up in the seam between the middle and outside blocker. This is the basic design. Adjustments are made based on attacker tendencies and each play. For example, if a ball is set outside the antenna, the line cannot be hit, so the line digger can move up and inside and cover tip.

ADVANTAGES: The white defensive scheme is very strong against a hard-hitting team. It takes advantage of a mobile defensive player in the middle back while reducing the responsibilities of the line and crosscourt diggers. It is strong against a crosscourt attack and requires little positional adjustments for the back row.

DISADVANTAGES: It is susceptible to most any tip and well-placed soft shot. There can be confusion between the offside blocker and the crosscourt digger.

Middle Back Up (Red—Figure 12.13)
Actually any designated back-row player can play "up" in this scheme. When the setter is in the back row, many teams put him or her up so that he or she is near the target area from which the offense is run. The setter, of course, makes the second contact. An obvious attack ploy is to tip the ball to the area where the setter is, thereby forcing the setter to handle the first contact rather than the set.

This scheme is designed to defend against the team that tips and hits off-speed.

ADVANTAGES: The red defensive scheme is strong against soft shots behind the block and in the middle. Strong combination counterattack is possible if the ball is controlled by any player but the setter.

DISADVANTAGES: Relying heavily on a stable, dependable block, the player up is susceptible to an uncontested middle-quick attack. The offside blocker must

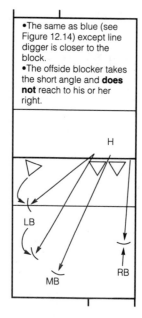

• The same as blue (see Figure 12.14) except line digger is closer to the block.
• The offside blocker takes the short angle and **does not** reach to his or her right.

Figure 12.12
White defensive scheme

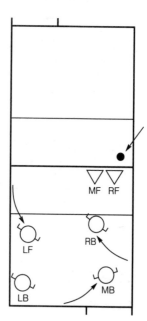

Figure 12.13
Red defensive scheme

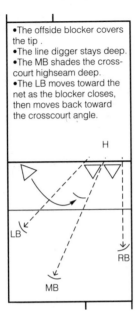

Figure 12.14

Blue defensive scheme

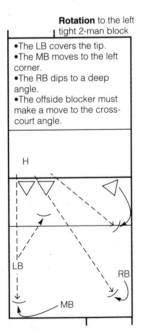

Rotation to the left
tight 2-man block

• The LB covers the tip.
• The MB moves to the left corner.
• The RB dips to a deep angle.
• The offside blocker must make a move to the crosscourt angle.

Figure 12.15

Rotation to the left with a tight, two-man block

drop deep to help in the crosscourt angle because there is one less deep back-row digger. The block must take the line because the line diggers need to cover the court vacated by the up player.

This defense is good to deploy on occasion, when there is a good chance the opponent will tip or hit an off-speed shot. If it is used all of the time, a good team can adjust its attack to its advantage.

Slide (Blue—Figure 12.14)

The offside blocker slides towards the point of attack, either to attempt to block (creating a three-player barricade) or to cover tip. The wing diggers take positions described in the white defense. The middle back reads and reacts as in the white defense. If three blockers are up, then the crosscourt digger can play closer to the net because the block shadow is greater. Likewise, the line digger can move up and cover the tip, because the three blockers are likely to shut down the potential line shot. The middle back roams and gets into the area most likely to be hit.

ADVANTAGES: The blue defense allows for tactical adjustments during play: for example, the option of blocking with three blockers and its related influence on the back-row deployment. Tips as well as hard shots are defended. Players strengths can be harnessed. For example, if the offside blocker is a weak digger but a strong blocker, the slide can get him or her involved in his or her strongest offering.

DISADVANTAGES: The area the offside blocker has vacated is susceptible to a tip or roll shot, putting pressure on the crosscourt digger to have to dig his or her area while being aware of the open space near the net. The offside blocker has to be consistent in making the slide move and either get into a good tip coverage posture or up to block. It can be difficult in the swirl of action.

Rotation (Figure 12.15)

This defense was the "in" defensive ploy during the 1980s. The idea behind the rotation is that it gets players moving so that they will flow with the play and not get stuck when the ball is attacked. In other words, it encourages movement. Basically, the diggers rotate toward the point of attack. The key word is *rotate,* not rush. The block moves normally, fronting the hitter. The line digger moves up and behind the middle blocker, stopping at about the 3-meter line. The middle back rotates *to the corner* and should be there when the ball is hit. The crosscourt digger rotates into a position that is in direct line from the point of attack to the crosscourt corner. The offside blocker moves back into the normal back-row crosscourt angle.

ADVANTAGES: It forces normally static players to move. It is strong against a line-hitting team if the middle-back player is a strong defender and gets into position. It covers tips and off-speed shots.

DISADVANTAGES: The more movement required, the more chance for players to be out of position when the ball is hit. It can be difficult to organize during a sustained rally. This defensive scheme is very susceptible to a line attack if players are not getting into consistent position. The area vacated by the offside blocker inside the 3-meter line is available for a tip or roll shot.

The four examples of defensive schemes are basic. There are many modifications based on game plans, player strengths or weaknesses, and coaching philosophies. When playing a defense, adhere to the principles and the strategies will be clear.

DESIGNING A SYSTEM

Any game of six-player volleyball is really made up of six little games. The unique rule of rotation requires each player to rotate every time the serve is earned by his or her team. Therefore, each time a team rotates, there is a different combination of players and positions. All of the playing system's starting positions are modified. Likewise, the opponent is rotating, creating different matchups of personnel. When designing systems of play, consider the rotation combinations and keep in mind the principle of *exposing your strengths and hiding your weaknesses.*

Tournament Play

13

Over the years, many methods have been created to determine the "number 1" team or individual in a particular sport. Single- and double-elimination tournaments are common to most sports, while single and double round-robin formats are common in the organization of leagues. Home-and-home scheduling is used in double round-robin leagues, in which each team plays opponents once at home and once at the opponent's home. The venerable Wimbledon Tennis Tournament is a single-elimination tournament in which a player losing a match is finished. The ultimate winner must win every match. Most college basketball and volleyball conferences (leagues) play home-and-home schedules. The NBA plays home-and-home games, with each team playing a few times on its home court and a few times on opponents' courts over an entire season.

Competitive formats provide equitable opportunities for teams and individuals to see where they stand compared with their peers over a given period of time. The drama of standings and the opportunities and risks of moving up or down enhance the competitive experience. Most people who engage in competitive sports enjoy the thrill of the hunt.

At every level, however, the spirit of competition can be dimmed when someone takes the consequences too seriously. Seldom has world history been altered by the results of athletics. Winning and losing are a part of life and should be kept in perspective. When kids play Little League baseball, they begin by enjoying the play. However, some well-meaning parents and coaches convey the message that losing is bad, humiliating, a blight on self-worth. When the emphasis is on the end product—winning or losing—and not on the *process* of doing one's best under any conditions, the true motivation to participate is skewed. Certainly, we must try our absolute best at everything we do; this should be a lifelong goal. It feels great to win, and it is disappointing to lose, but seldom devastating. It is virtually an art form when two equal opponents meet and give their best. The intensity of focus is on tactics and the corresponding skills. No one whines. They just play. Finally, someone wins and someone loses that particular contest. If great effort is put forth by both principles, basic sportsmanship through mutual respect is demonstrated and no one's self-worth is impugned. It is as it should be: Compete, play, and, win or lose, move on to the next day and game. If the excitement and enjoyment is not there for you, find another activity.

Discussing the merits of competition often makes one wax philosophical. A description of various competitive formats follows.

POOLS

Any of the combinations of numbers and genders in team makeup can play in pools. Although water can be a medium for volleyball play, the pools discussed here are of the dry variety. Pool play that lasts days, weeks, or months can be applied in leagues. College athletics call them conferences; in the pros they're called divisions. Pools usually are identified with tournaments that are shorter in duration than leagues. Pool play requires at least six teams that are then divided into two pools of three. There is no maximum number that can play in a pool. However, if there are more than six teams, scheduling in a restricted time block can become logistically difficult. Before organizing a competition, you need to understand some basic terms:

Tournament. This is an organized series of games among several individual teams in any given sport to determine a linear ranking.

Pool. This is a grouping of teams or individuals determined by a random draw or criteria-based seeding. Two or more pools can be organized to form a tournament.

Seeding. In formal tournaments where specific criteria determine the relative strengths of the participating teams or individuals, an effort is made to balance the stronger and weaker teams in the pools so that everyone has relatively equal playing schedules.

Round-robin. Within a pool (or league, division, or conference), every team plays each other. Most tournaments have *single round-robins,* in which each team plays each other once. A league will often have a *double round-robin,* in which each team plays each other twice in a *home-and-home* format—that is, one game is played at one team's home base and the other at the opponent's home base.

Crisscross final. When pool play is completed and rankings are established, the second-place team from pool A plays the first-place team from pool B and the first-place team from pool A plays the second-place team from pool B. The winners from these two matches play for the championship, and the losers play for third and fourth place. The crisscross can apply down the ranks of the pools. The third and fourth teams in each pool crisscross for positions of fifth through eighth place in the tournament.

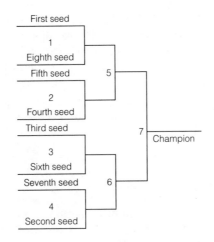

Figure 13.1

Single-elimination bracket for eight teams

Single elimination. Teams or individuals are seeded into a *bracket,* or an organizational map of a championship match. If a team wins, it continues to the next destination. If a team loses, it is out (Figure 13.1). This format can be used in two ways: to accommodate a large number of teams or individuals (the NCAA Division-I basketball tournament leading to the Final Four is a well-publicized example) or to accommodate a tournament with more than two pools. (Instead of a crisscross final, teams are seeded into a single-elimination final.)

Double elimination. This format is divided into a *winners' bracket* and a *losers' bracket.* If teams or individuals continue to win, they continue on as in the single-elimination format. However, if a team loses one time, it goes into a losers' bracket, which is basically a back-road map back to the championship final (Figure 13.2). But if a team loses in the losers' bracket, it is out. Double-elimination tournaments can be time-consuming. Many state high school associations combine a single- and double-elimination format (Figure 13.3). To ensure that teams have at least two matches, they provide for a second match, even if a team loses its first competition. However, unlike the double-elimination format, a team that loses once can no longer have a chance at playing in the championship.

When a team in any tournament is not playing while others are, it is known as drawing a BYE. Many people new to tournament play wonder what team BYE is when they see the schedule. It simply means that you are not playing in that time slot.

These are the basic organizational formats. There are other, creative formats that must take into account varying numbers of teams, playing venues, and time limits when organizing tournaments that are as fair to all participants as possible and interesting to players and fans. Graphic examples of these formats will be presented in the following sections.

Begin

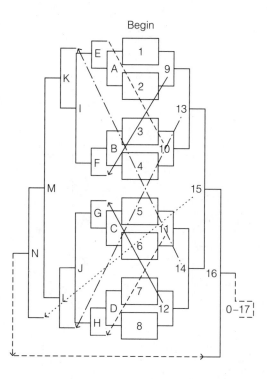

End of opening round*

Winner	1	to	9	Loser	1	to	A
	2	to	9		2	to	A
	3	to	10		3	to	B
	4	to	10		4	to	B
	5	to	11		5	to	C
	6	to	11		6	to	C
	7	to	12		7	to	D
	8	to	12		8	to	D

Winners' bracket, first round

Winner	9	to	13	Loser	9	to	F
	10	to	13		10	to	E
	11	to	14		11	to	H
	12	to	12		12	to	G

Losers' bracket, first round

Winner	A	to	E
	B	to	F
	C	to	G
	D	to	H

Winners' bracket, second round

Winner	13	to	15	Loser	13	to	L
	14	to	15		14	to	K

Losers' bracket, second round

Winner	E	to	I
	F	to	I
	G	to	J
	H	to	J

Winners' bracket, second round

Winner 15 to 16   Loser   15 to N

Losers' bracket, third round

Winner I to K
         J to L

Losers' bracket, fourth round

Winner K to M
         L to M

Losers' bracket, fifth round

Winner M to N

Losers' bracket, final round

Winner N to 16

Championship match

If the victor is the winner of Match 15, then that team is champion. If the victor is the winner of match N, then it is the first loss for the match-15 winner. Therefore, the 0–17 match/ game is played to determine the ultimate champion.

*Any team losing a match after the opening round is out.

Figure 13.2

Double-elimination bracket for 16 teams

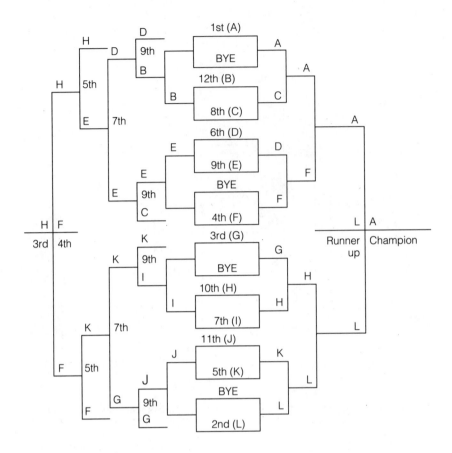

Team	Place
A	1st
L	2nd
H	3rd
F	4th
E	5th
K	5th
D	7th
G	7th
B	9th
A	9th
I	9th
J	9th

Figure 13.3   Single-double elimination bracket for 12 teams

ORGANIZING A TOURNAMENT

So what? you say. Well, perhaps, a few examples will shed some light on the complexities of organizing a competition. Let's say that you are a member of a family whose roots can be traced up to prehistoric time, a family who has held reunions ever since the landing at Plymouth Rock. You are appointed social director. You must organize a tournament. Because this book is about volleyball, we will go through the steps of organizing a volleyball tournament here. However, these steps are applicable to any number of athletic activities.

The first thing you must do is send out a notice describing the activity (Figure 13.4), for example, a coed, four-player (two males, two females) grass tournament. Depending on the number of teams you choose, use a round-robin pool play with a crisscross final.

When you know how many teams you have, organize the tournament. For illustration purposes, we will organize a ten-team tournament and a fifteen-team tournament.

When organizing an event, you must consider the facilities that are needed or available, the time block assigned, and the number of teams. When playing indoors, the time constraints and facility limitations are much more restrictive. Gyms have just so many playable courts, and scheduling can be a hassle and expensive. Outdoor tournaments are much more accommodating in terms of space. There are lots of grassy fields and sandy beaches. However, you must have enough court standards and nets to make courts. Also, weather can be a limiting factor for the less hearty.

Time becomes a factor if you are renting facilities or if daylight is limited. Our illustrations will assume grass courts in a park during July, so time and space are of no concern. You have equipment to set up three courts.

Ten-Team Tournament

There will be two pools of five teams. Because there are no criteria for seeding, make the pools as balanced as possible based on your knowledge of the players involved. Assign each team a name for the purpose of identification and to add some spirit to the event. After registrations are in and before a schedule is determined, organize as follows:

Blue Pool	*Gold Pool*
1. Bashibazouk	1. Piblokto
2. Red Tide	2. The Future
3. Oldies	3. Travesty
4. Yikes	4. *Rodents Under Net*
5. JugRnot	5. Pox

Tournament Announcement Form

What: (Name of tournament)

Date: (Day[s]), date[s])

Time: (Starting time, time blocks for competition, finals starting time)

Where: (Location, address, directions or map)

Who: (Specify who is invited and what, if any, restrictions)

Format: (Describe the type of tournament and how many games/matches each team is guaranteed)

Awards: (Describe awards—team and individual—if any)

Officials: (If they are provided or if teams need to bring a certified official or provide linespersons and scorers and so on)

Other: (Food, drinks, housing, T-shirts, any unique programs, limit on number of teams, problems, schedule oddities, embellishments)

Cost: (Entry fee and accepted method of payment)

Deadline: (Absolute deadline when entries and fee must be in. Give yourself adequate time to make adjustments to the number of teams)

Contact: (Name, address, and phone number to send entries or to direct questions)

Figure 13.4 Sample volleyball tournament announcement

Each pool is scheduled on the following formula:

team 1 vs team 2	team 5 vs team 3
team 3 vs team 4	team 4 vs team 1
team 5 BYE	team 2 BYE
team 2 vs team 4	team 3 vs team 1
team 1 vs team 5	team 5 vs team 2
team 3 BYE	team 4 BYE
team 4 vs team 5	
team 2 vs team 3	
team 1 BYE	

Each pool will use this formula. The team drawing the BYE will referee the matches in their pool. The team numbers correspond with the team names; for example, G3 is Travesty, B1 Bashibazouk.

Using three courts presents a scheduling problem. If there were four, scheduling two five-team pools would be obvious and easy. However, the object here is to present a common scheduling situation. The following solution can be used:

Court 1	*Court 2*	*Court 3*
B1 vs B2	G1 vs G2	B3 vs B4
G3 vs G4	B1 vs B5	G1 vs G5
B2 vs B4	G2 vs G4	B5 vs B3
G4 vs G5	B4 vs B5	G2 vs G3
B2 vs B3	G5 vs G3	B4 vs B1
G4 vs G1	B3 vs B1	G5 vs G2
B5 vs B2	—	G3 vs G1

Two pools and three courts can be difficult to balance BYEs and playing teams. When scheduling, try to be as equitable as possible when considering play-to-rest ratios. The above example has a couple of teams with three matches in a row and two rests back to back. Usually, in any format, a team thinks it's at a disadvantage only if it's losing.

The next problem to solve is to put the format into a *time block*. There are several ways to control the match length: Play fast score (rally point, described in Chapter 2); play two games to 15 points in each round; reduce the number of points per game to 11; or play timed games. If two-out-of-three-game matches are played, a minimum of 1 hour of playing time is required for 15-point games. If a third game is necessary, it must be a rally-point game. This excludes warm-ups but includes the potential for a third game. Teams should warm up off the playing court. Understand that if there is no time limit, matches could last longer than 1 hour, throwing a tightly scheduled tournament behind time. You must determine whether timed games, reduced-point games, all rally-score games, or increasing the time block for each match is most appropriate for your situation.

Remember also that after pool play there will be a crisscross final with two more matches. If you needed to limit the time used for the final, you could have the two pool champions only play for the tournament championship—known as a *straight-cross final*—and thereby reduce the championship match to one.

Below are a couple examples of tightly scheduled tournaments. Note that these schedules assume that everything goes as planned.

7 rounds of pool play × 1 hour each	=	7 hours
Crisscross final—2 matches × 1 hour	=	2 hours
Assume ½-hour's rest between pool play, semis, and finals	=	1 hour
	TOTAL	10 hours

Therefore, if the tournament begins at 9:00 A.M., pool play concludes at 4:00 P.M. The semifinals begin at 4:30 and finish at 5:30. The finals begin at 6:00. It works. But it is more appropriate for the hard-core volleyball player.

The next formula calculates the time for a two-out-of-three-game, 11-point-game match:

7 rounds of pool play × 30 minutes each	= 3½ hours
Crisscross final—2 matches × 30 minutes each	= 1 hour
Assume 15 minutes' rest between pool play, semis, and finals	= ½ hour
TOTAL	5 hours

If the tournament starts at 10:00 A.M. and there is an hour's lunch break, the tournament will be over at 4:00 P.M.

Elimination tournaments defeat the purpose of social competition because losing means being finished. However, an elimination final coupled with a pool-play tournament can be effective for social play as outlined in the next example.

Fifteen-Team Tournament

The pool formula described in the ten-team example applies here also because we are dealing with multiples of five. Simply add a third pool (red pool). The problem is keeping the time block manageable. If there are three courts, then each pool has a court. It will require ten time slots to complete the round-robin with one court per pool. If you have two courts per pool, five slots will do. Trying to secure enough space and equipment may be the best way to solve the time problem. Assuming this option is not possible, you need to limit each round to 45 minutes. You can either play two-out-of-three-game matches using rally-point scoring or play two 15-point games only each round.

***The Fifteen-Team, Three-Court Round-robin Schedule (all courts are on
same schedule)***

8:00 A.M.	1 vs 2	11:45 A.M.	2 vs 3
8:45 A.M.	3 vs 4	12:30 P.M.	1 vs 4
9:30 A.M.	1 vs 5	1:15 P.M.	5 vs 2
10:15 A.M.	2 vs 4	2:00 P.M.	3 vs 1
11:00 A.M.	4 vs 5	2:45 P.M.	5 vs 3

Again, it is difficult to balance play and rest ratios.

The Play-offs   A crisscross final won't work. A straight-cross final won't work.
So what works? A single elimination (Figure 13.5).

The records of each of the three pool champions are compared. The pool champion with the best record gets the first seed; the pool champion with the second-
best record, the second seed; and the pool champion with the third-best record, the
third seed. The records of the second-place teams from each of the three pools are
then compared. The team with the best second-place record is seeded fourth; the
team with the second-best second-place record is seeded fifth; and the team with
the third-best second-place record is seeded sixth.

Breaking Ties   What if two teams from different pools have the same *match*
win-loss record? There is a standard formula for breaking ties:

- The team with best *game* win-loss record is ranked higher.
- If they are still tied, then the team with the best ratio of points won to points
  lost is ranked higher.
- If they are still tied, then flip a coin. The winner of the flip is ranked higher.

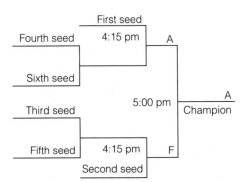

Figure 13.5   Single-elimination bracket for six teams

THE OBJECTIVE IS TO PLAY

Tournaments can heighten the joy of playing. They can be highly organized or created on the spot. Add prizes or consequences appropriate to the situation. Many people who have never really played in a tournament format will be thrilled to be part of a team that works and plays together toward a goal. The inherent drama of matches being played simultaneously on surrounding courts enhances the interest in the event. The feeling of camaraderie among teammates as well as among all of the tournament's participants is special. Anyone who has run in an organized 10K can identify the feeling. Doing one's very best is the glue of mutual respect among all players. Participating in an event like this is as enjoyable as eating a luscious cake; winning is only the icing.

The Many Varieties
of Volleyball

14

The ways volleyball can be played are only limited by our imagination. The traditional player combinations of volleyball were discussed in Chapter 11. This book also covered the established rules, competitions, and, in some cases, associations that govern organized play. But why be hampered by tradition? Why not create new applications? In this chapter, we will explore optional scoring systems and rules as well as unique and bizarre venues and formats for playing volleyball.

SCORING SYSTEMS

The classic six-player volleyball, with its side-out scoring, is unique among sports. A volleyball match can be brief or lengthy. If one team overwhelms the other, a three-out-of-five-game match can be completed in less than 45 minutes. Likewise, if two teams are balanced and are equally capable of preventing the other team from scoring often, a match can last longer than 3 hours. Having no time limit changes the mental attitude toward play: You can't run out the clock. You must score the winning points in each game as well as the match. Racket sports including tennis, racquetball, and badminton are similar, but there are no team sports without some sort of time limit. The closest popular sport is baseball.

The recent inclusion of rally-point scoring (or fast scoring, in which a point is scored on every play) in the deciding game of a match by the FIVB is an attempt to control the time block of a match. FIVB rules also put a 17-point cap on each game. The objective is to encourage televised coverage of volleyball by controlling the length of a match.

Another element of volleyball that makes it unique is that it is a rebound sport. A guarantee accompanies each serve—the guarantee that there will be a measurable consequence to each play. It's kind of like white-water canoeing: Once you enter the fury of the rapids, you can't start over. Once the serve is in the air (and the canoe is on the water), you are committed; each play has a consequence.

The upshot is that volleyball, in its present, traditional form, is unique and extremely interesting. Changing the way points are scored can control the time of play, modify the focus of a game, and redesign the tactics. Scoring systems can alter the mental as well as the physical workout. Below are types and descriptions of scoring systems:

Side-out scoring (traditional scoring). Points can only be scored by a team when it is serving.

Rally-point scoring (fast scoring). Points are scored on every play regardless of which team is serving.

Wash scoring. Two or more "little points" must be consecutively scored to score one "big point." A game is won when a predetermined number of big points is scored. When one team cannot string the required number of consecutive little points in a series of play, it is known as a "wash."

Bongo scoring. Similar to wash scoring, bongo scoring requires the consecutive accumulation of a predetermined number of little points. However, tallying the right number of little points does not yield a big point. It merely gives you the opportunity to try and score a bongo point. In other words, the *next* play is for a bongo. If the team that earned the chance is stopped on the bongo attempt, the consecutive accumulation of little points starts again. If the team does score on the bongo attempt, then they earn the bongo. A game is decided on accumulating a predetermined number of bongo points.

Wash and bongo scoring come out of U.S. National Men's Team drills, where the object is to train the team to play consistently over a long period of time while maintaining momentum and dealing with the inherent frustrations of volleyball. Over time, it has been found that these scoring systems are challenging and lots of fun and can be applied to a variety of games.

UNIQUE TOURNAMENT FORMATS

Roller Derby

No, you don't play volleyball on wheels or blades. Classic roller derby (professional wrestling on skates) features two opposing stables, each with a men's team and a women's team. In a game (match? meet? epic?), the men "play" against the men and the women against the women. The score accumulates as the teams alternate time on the court.

Even though the "sport" of roller derby begs for skeptics, the competitive format has merit for volleyball. Each volleyball team is made up of a men's squad and a women's squad. A game is played up to 75 points (or a number divisable by 5). Traditional and rally-point scoring are the best options for scoring. The team winning the coin flip can choose serve and side *or* which squad starts the game. Obviously, if team A chooses to start their women, then team B must also. The net is adjusted to the correct height (2.43 meters for men and 2.24 meters for women). The chosen squads play until the cumulative score is divisible by 10. For example, team A's women take a 7 to 3 lead. Now the men's squads take the court. The net is adjusted to the proper height, and the men continue the game. When the score again reaches a number divisible by 10 (for example, 11 to 9) the women's squads return. The game continues until the designated number of points for a win is reached by one of the teams. The roller derby is a great way to use men and women in one game but play two different games. The strategy of matching up a team's squads with the opponent's and trying to figure out which squad is best to have on the court near the end is fascinating.

Handicap Draw

A wide range of skills and varying levels of experience are often exhibited in classes, informal get-togethers, camps, YMCA noon sessions, and so on. The dilemma is how to include everyone and to have an enjoyable time. The handicap draw attempts to balance the disparity. Each player is given a handicap. Unlike golf, the better a volleyball player is, the higher the handicap. For example, the top players in a group will carry a handicap of 8; the least experienced players, a 1. Some criteria need to be established to determine what handicap a player should receive. They could be based on experience, physical attributes, competitive success, or a combination. After the handicaps have been determined for the participants, teams are drawn blindly. For example, team A draws six players with the following handicaps: 6, 8, 8, 4, 1, 2 (total: 29). Team B draws players with the handicaps 1, 1, 8, 6, 6, 2 (total: 24). At the beginning of each game of the match, team B has 5 points and team A has 0 points to compensate for the 5-point difference between the teams' total handicaps.

A tournament can be organized with a predetermined number of matches. Teams are redrawn prior to each match. Players get 3 points for a match win and 1 point for each game won. For example, team A beats team B three games to two. Each member of team A gets 3 points for the match win plus 1 point for each game won (total: 6 points). Team-B players each get 1 point for each game they won (total: 2 points). After several matches and many combinations of players, there is a ranking of individual players. The handicaps make it challenging for the experienced player and allow the newcomer or less-talented player to participate.

Stable

Most likely the sports term "stable" comes from horse racing. The term has been expanded to mean several race cars or boats owned by one person or several boxers or players managed by one person or group, to name a few examples. In volleyball, a stable of teams, playing a variety of competitive formats, can be organized into an overall tournament program. For example, a stable tournament will consist of men's and women's doubles, coed doubles, men's and women's triples, coed fours, and men's and women's sixes—a total of eight different competitions within the tournament. Each stable can enter two doubles teams in each of the three doubles competitions (men's, women's, and coed), two triples teams in each triples competition, two coed teams in the fours, and one team in each sixes competition. Therefore, if a stable has six women and six men, they can all participate in each competition. If a stable has more players, then the tournament format allows for plenty of action for every person.

The tournament winner is the stable that has accumulated the most points throughout the various competitions. Potential points won at each level depend somewhat on how many teams are involved. However, scoring is progressive, as shown in the following example:

Doubles:	1st	10 points	Fours:	1st	20 points
	2nd	7		2nd	15
	3rd	5		3rd	12
	4th	3		4th	9
	5th	1		5th	7
Triples:	1st	12 points	Sixes:	1st	40 points
	2nd	9		2nd	30
	3rd	7		3rd	25
	4th	5		4th	18
	5th	3		5th	15

The stable that accumulates the most points throughout the tournament wins.

It is important to note that each player can only play on one team in each category of competition. For example, a player on a men's doubles team cannot play on the coed doubles team.

This tournament can span a weekend or ten weeks, depending on the numbers, facilities, available time, and level of fanaticism of the players. Whatever the time block, stable tournaments are social, dramatic, and great fun, and they encourage teamwork and support.

Progressive

This tournament program is similar to stables in that it involves several variations of volleyball. It is a good event for players with a wide range of abilities and little familiarity with each other. In party terms, the progressive tournament is the equivalent of a "mixer."

One-on-One   Start with a narrow-court one-on-one tournament, playing fast-score, timed games to keep everything on schedule. Divide each court into two or three narrow courts. Three, one-on-one games can be played on a single regulation volleyball court; however, Figure 14.1 illustrates a two-lane setup. Play 3-minute fast-score games. At the end of a 3-minute time block, winners move one court north and losers move one court south. The object is to move as far north as possible. A player who wins on the court furthest north stays. Likewise, the player

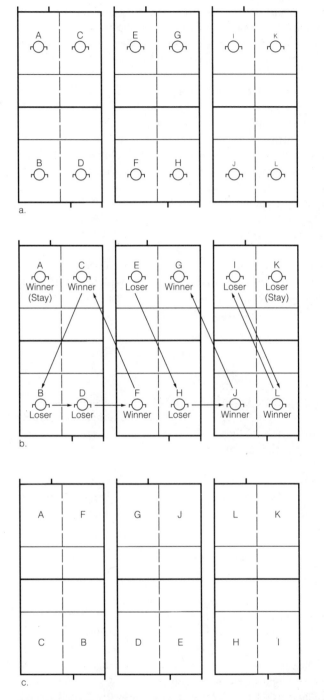

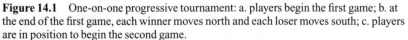

Figure 14.1 One-on-one progressive tournament: a. players begin the first game; b. at the end of the first game, each winner moves north and each loser moves south; c. players are in position to begin the second game.

who loses on the furthest court south stays. Everyone else moves one way or the other (Figures 14.1b and 14.1c). When time is called, the play in progress is completed and counts. A win in a tied score goes to the player who got the point first. For example, in a 5-5 tie, if player A scored 5 before player B, then player A wins.

This segment of the tournament is played in a predetermined number of timed games. The number of games must allow the players starting at the most southern point to work their way up to the most northern point. There should be enough games to allow for a player to lose one or two games and still be able to win the competition. Players should begin in inverse order of their ability levels, if they are known. The best players start in the south and the less talented in the north. There is a linear ranking of players at the end of the one-on-one.

A note is appropriate at this point: Be geographically sensitive. If this tournament is played in Florida, "moving south" may be preferred. Therefore, reverse the example. The game can also be played east-west depending on who's playing.

Doubles   The second segment of the progressive tournament is a doubles competition. The teams are determined by matching the best with the worst based on the final standings in the one-on-one competition. For example, if there are 12 players, the doubles teams are made up as follows:

1 and 12	4 and 9
2 and 11	5 and 8
3 and 10	6 and 7

The doubles competition is played on half-courts. The games should be longer than the one-on-one games—for example, 6-minute games instead of 3-minute games. Again, teams move north if they win and south if they lose. Each team's starting position is determined by a blind draw.

Fours   The third segment of the tournament is a fours competition. Played on a full court, the format depends on how many teams are available. Using the 12-player example, there are now 3 teams. The teams are determined by the same formula used in doubles:

1st and 6th

2nd and 5th

3rd and 4th

A good 3-team format is a fast-score, little game–big game competition. A predetermined number of points, say 75, is set for winning the big game. Little games are played to 5 fast-score points. When a team scores 5 points in a little game, it stays on the court and the team that was off the court replaces the losing team. The losing team accumulates whatever points it scored and adds them to its total score. The big game is won when one team scores a total of 75 points, as the following list shows:

Little game 1: team A versus team B (team C is off)
Team B wins the first game 5-3 and stays on the court to play team C.
Score: team A, 3; team B, 5; team C, 0.

Little game 2: team B versus team C (team A is off)
Team B wins again 5-2 and stays on the court to play team A in the next
little game. Score: team A, 3; team B, 10; team C, 2.

Little game 3: team A versus team B (team C is off)
Team A wins 5-1, sending team B off the court. Team C comes on for the
next game. Score: team A, 8; team B, 11; team C, 2.

Little game 4: team A versus team C (team B is off)
Team C wins 5-4, sending team A off the court. Team B returns to the
court. Score: team A, 12; team B, 11; team C, 7.

The competition continues until one team gains the predetermined total points to
win the big game.

Sixes The fourth and final segment of the progressive tournament is a 6-player
competition. We still have 12 players. The players have accumulated individual
points as a result of their finishes in the three segments already played. In the one-
on-one, each player gets the number of points represented by his or her position in
inverse order. In other words, the first-place player gets 12 points, the second-
place player gets 11, the third-place player gets 10, and so on down to 1. In doubles,
the first-place player through the sixth-place player receive the following points,
respectively: 12, 10, 8, 6, 4, and 2. The fours competition is scored 12, 8, and 4,
first place through third place.

Players are placed on one of two teams using a serpentine method. (If players
are tied, a flip of the coin determines who goes first.) The serpentine is

Team A	*Team B*
1st	2nd
3rd	4th
5th	6th
7th	8th
9th	10th
11th	12th

In the six-player segment, a standard 3-out-of-5-game match is a good conclusion to the tournament. Use any scoring system that best serves time and interest.
Each player on the winning team gets 12 points plus 2 points per game won. The
losing team's players each get 6 points plus 2 points per game won.

The player who wins the most points over the entire progressive tournament is
the champ. This activity does not need to be played for individual points. The
finishes in each segment can be used just for determining the makeup of the next
competition's teams.

Jim Bjerring's Narrow-Court Doubles

Jim Bjerring, former assistant coach for the Canadian Women's National Volleyball Team and a professor at the University of British Columbia, developed a volleyball tournament format that provides a linear ranking of players at the conclusion of the competition. It has been used as an evaluation of volleyball skills in team tryout situations but can stand alone as a great competitive activity. A computer-generated schedule ensures that every player plays *with everyone once and against everyone twice*. Standings at the end of the tournament are determined by games won and lost. Ties are broken by points for and against. For example, if two players are tied with 7 wins, the tie is broken by taking the player who has the greater difference between positive points and negative points. If player A has 7 wins and scored a total of 37 points and lost a total of 29 points, he or she has a +8. Player B also has 7 wins and scored 42 points and lost 35 points, giving him or her a +7. Player A wins.

The tournament can be played by various numbers of players with different levels of skills. Games are timed to keep everyone on schedule. A regular volleyball court is split in half, creating two courts. Therefore, if you have three regulation courts available, they can be retooled into six narrow courts.

The rules are basic volleyball rules: Players must rotate, each series can have up to three contacts, and so on. However, special rules can be used. For example: games can be timed; a team can win by one point; if there is a tie, the team that arrives at the tied point first wins; a player cannot go into an adjoining active court to play a ball (it's interference); the ball can cross the net anywhere as long as it lands in the narrow court.

If there are enough antennae available, a third one is attached at center net, with the two outside antennae in their normal locations. The ball must then pass between the antennae marking the narrow court.

For complete details on how to run the Bjerring or linear-ranking tournaments, order the book *Linear Ranking Tournaments* by Michael P. Fleming, published by his own Acorn Company, P.O. Box 663, Mead, Washington, 99021. Coach Fleming is the authority on linear-ranking tournaments. His book covers every situation—varying numbers of players, numbers of courts, and time requirements. His book thoroughly covers tournament organization, rules, formulas, and forms. This book is a must if you intend to go into teaching or coaching or simply plan to run your company's leagues.

BIZARRE VENUES

Some form of volleyball can be played virtually anywhere. Do you have a living room and a coffee table? Move anything that is breakable and valuable. Center the coffee table in the room. Use a sturdy, relatively round balloon or a beach ball. Play singles, doubles, or triples. Players sit and scoot around on their posteriors to play the "ball." The ball can be hit off the wall (which, when you think about it, is appropriate), the ceiling, lamps, furniture, or other objects. Points or side-outs are scored only when the ball hits the floor or the team cannot return fire over the "net" in three contacts. The 1976 Canadian Olympic Team held an over-the-coffee-table doubles tournament in the coach's living room. It was a great social event. A good time was had by all. And, the living room survived.

Do you live in a college dorm? Over-the-bed volleyball will do. If you have bunk beds that can split the room, the game can be played standing. No jumping is allowed, especially if the ceiling is low.

Some people have been known to put eyebolts into their living room or rec room walls so that a badminton net can be strung up to allow the game to be played standing. And when these fanatics are ready to sell their homes, they can promote this unique fixture as a selling point to the next indoor-sports fanatic.

Following are a few variations on volleyball venues and games:

Walleyball. Walleyball is a copyrighted game that has its own association, leagues and championships, and formal rules. It is a game played in a racquetball/handball court using either a regular volleyball or a special Walleyball. It is a mixture of racquetball and handball—in which there are wall and ceiling shots—and volleyball skills. It is very popular at athletic and health clubs.

Tennis volleyball. Basically, this game is tennis played with a volleyball and without a racket. If singles play, there is just one contact—after the ball bounces once off the serve—on each side to return the ball over the net. If doubles teams are playing, there are two contacts per side: the first is after one bounce off the serve and the second is direct from the person making the first contact, that is, no second bounce is allowed. Players can jump and spike.

The game is a superb workout. This game is modified in Brazil so that players can use only their feet. It's far removed from any volleyball skills but is an interesting variation.

Mud volleyball. When you hear those radio commercials promoting tractor pulls in the mud ("Muuudd Runninnn . . . The winners get muddy. The losers get *really* MUUUDDYYY. Come on down and watch 'em WAL-LLOOOWWW!"), don't you want to just get down and dirty? Since most of us don't own tractors, we can strive for a similar thrill playing mud volleyball. Play with any number of people, choose any kind of tournament, use any scoring system, and use an old ball. Make sure there are no rocks in the playing area and that the material is good, clean mud. As gross as it may sound, mud volleyball is pure fun.

Water volleyball. There are several private clubs and families with swimming pools who set up volleyball nets from one side to the other, making the pool a volleyball court. The water is the floor, and you can use standard volleyball rules or modify them if you wish. Basically, the players' heads stick out of the "floor" and the legs and arms propel the body up to make contact with the ball. The net height is approximately a meter above the water. Any number can play. Be aware that there is a significant disadvantage for players in the deep end of the pool. Ideally, the water line should be at the players' necks when their toes are touching the bottom of the pool. Because players will vary in height and pools normally have slanting bottoms, try to make the game as equitable as possible. For example, have teams change sides every 5 points.

Snow. Are you really nuts? Play in waist-deep snow. This is a cleaner, colder version of mud volleyball and features the inherent resistance of water volleyball. It can be played with any number of people, using any scoring system, and in any competitive format. Be sure to have a lodge with a roaring fire and hot showers waiting for you. It's a great activity for a ski weekend.

Solid net. Regular volleyball nets allow players to see the opponents and their intentions. Take away the view and you have a different game. Throw a blanket over a regular net, or play over a wall or a backyard fence. It keeps players alert and encourages sneaky play. Interesting!

SUMMARY

The objective of this chapter is to stimulate creative thinking in using volleyball as a life sport. These are just a few ideas. The best ones haven't been thought of yet. So a question remains: Why are you still reading this? Get out and create! Get some friends together and play! Join a team! A club! A class! Don't just read about it, *play* it! Serve it up!

Sample 2-Hour Practice

This is a sample practice with a primary focus on hitting as it relates to ball control. Quicks and blocking get attention also. This practice will benefit fitness because it is a high-movement practice with plenty of jumping. There are natural intervals of intense action. The overload principle is in effect, especially in the gauntlet drill, in which the gauntlet hitters have little recovery in their runs. The back rows on each side get *active rest* because they are in the back court longer than normal and don't jump. However, they do get good ball-control practice. The overall emphasis of the practice is working on the transition part of the game, which is where most teams break down.

12 minutes   Warm-up

Jog with easy approach spike jumps and block jumps (3 minutes); serve and follow (3 minutes); stretch (4 minutes); do accelerations (2 minutes).

18 minutes   One-on-one

Play nine 2-minute, fast-score games—winners move north, losers move south (see Chapter 14). *Focus:* ball control.

15 minutes   Deep-court exchange

Two groups of six each are divided into four groups of three. Exchange after the ball crosses the net to the other side (see Chapter 7). *Focus:* ball control, related movements, and coordination with teammates.

45 minutes   Gauntlet hitting

A team divides into groups of three. Each group is made up of specialized playing responsibilities. Two groups are on one side of the net, making a team of six. One group is in the back row of the other court and receives serve, covers, and plays defense. The other group on that side of the net runs the gauntlet and must execute three quicks, two left-sides, two right-sides, and two *X*s to complete one run. They must successfully complete two runs before rotating. The team of six blocks and plays defense, trying to prevent the run. The gauntlet team can hit any option at any time, but once a target number is attained, a further success of that option does not count. Once the gauntlet is successfully completed, the groups "wave" through (Figure A.1). The action

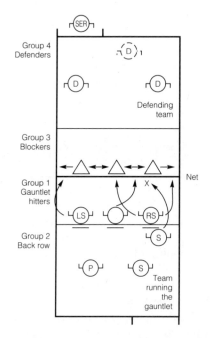

Figure A.1 Gauntlet hitting: After group 1 successfully completes their attack assignment, they wave to the other side of the net, replacing group 3. Group 3 replaces group 4. Group 4 replaces group 2. Group 2 replaces group 1.

starts with a serve. After a ball is dead, a free ball is thrown in from a coach to the gauntlet side of the net. The coach restarts a sequence with a serve when he or she sees fit. A gauntlet point can be scored in any series of plays. *Focus:* transition hitting and matchup blocking.

30 minutes   *Two-out-of-three-game, fast-score match*

Two six-player teams play a fast-score match. A successful quick attack is worth 2 points. *Focus:* quick attack and block response.

12 minutes   *Cool-down*

Repeat the warm-up in reverse order.

Resources

Associations and Organizations

Acorn Company (Mike Fleming)
P.O. Box 663
Mead, WA 99021
(509) 466-3472

American Beach Volleyball League (CE Sports and
 Entertainment)
6921 B Woodley Avenue
Van Nuys, CA 91406
(818) 782-8920

American Volleyball Coaches Association (AVCA)
1227 Lake Plaza Drive, Suite B
Colorado Springs, CO 80906
(719) 576-7777

Association of Volleyball Professionals (AVP)
100 Corporate Pointe, Suite 100
Culver City, CA 90230
(213) 337-4842

Baden Sports, Inc.
34114 21st Avenue South
Federal Way, WA 98003
(206) 925-0500

Federation Internationale de Volley-ball (FIVB)
Avenue de la Gare 12
CH-1001 Lausanne, Switzerland

National Association of Girls and Women in Sport
 (NAGWS)
1900 Association Drive
Reston, VA 22091

National Strength and Conditioning Association
 (NSACA)
P.O. Box 81410
Lincoln, NE 68501

Sports Imports
P.O. Box 21108
Columbus, OH 43221
(614) 771-0246

The United States Volleyball Association (USVBA)
3595 East Fountain Boulevard
Colorado Springs, CO 80910-1740
(719) 637-8300

Women's Professional Volleyball Association
 (WPVA)
400 Corporate Pointe, Suite 725
Culver City, CA 90230
(213) 215-2969

Magazines

Volleyball Magazine
 Editorial office:
 950 Calle Amanecer, Suite C
 Box 3010
 San Clemente, CA 92672
 (714) 492-7873

 Subscriptions:
 Dept. Volleyball
 P.O. Box 566
 Mt. Morris, IL 61054
 (815) 734-6309

Volleyball Monthly
P.O. Box 3137
San Luis Obispo, CA 93403
(805) 541-2294

Volley Tech
Philippka-Verlag
Konrad Honig, P.B. 6540
D-4400 Munster, Germany

VolleyWorld
FIVB
12 Avenue de la Gare
1001 Lausanne, Switzerland

Camps

In late winter and early spring, Volleyball Monthly provides a comprehensive list of volleyball camps for players.

Instructional Videos

Truckee River Studios (TRS)
P.O. Box 1040
Alamo, CA 94507
1-800-824-0477

Glossary

Acceleration Increasing the speed throughout the attack approach from the first step to ball contact.

Attack The offensive category comprising the tactical and technical skills of terminating the ball on the opponent's side of the net.

Attack (or spike) angle The linear direction in which the spiker hits the ball.

Back-row set A set placed so that a player in the back row can take off from behind the 3-meter line and attack.

Backslide A common attack pattern in which a spiker begins his or her approach in front of the setter and uses either a one- or two-foot takeoff and drifts or broad jumps past and behind the setter to hit the ball.

Being compact Keeping the arms and legs within control of the torso while playing the ball and avoiding flailing off balance at the ball.

Big area The greatest portion of the court covered by one passer during the serve receive.

Block The attempt of one or more players on one team to deflect an opponent's spiked attack back onto the opponent's court, slow down the spike so that a back-row defender on the blocker's team can pass the ball, or channel the spike into a defended area.

Block shadow The area in the court behind the block where the ball cannot be spiked with high velocity.

Brake step The final step of the approach that stops and positions a player in a balanced and stable position to play a ball.

Bumping Slang for serve receive.

Commit block Usually used against a quick hitter. A blocker jumps with a hitter before knowing if that hitter is going to be set.

Control block The blockers deflect or slow down a hard-hit attack so that a back-row defender can handle the next contact.

Dark serve Slang for a very deceptive serve that dips and moves away from the receivers.

Dedicate block A tactic in which one blocker is deployed in front of a predicted point of attack or in front of a specific hitter before the ball is put into play.

Dig The technique of retrieving a hard-hit ball.

Dig lips A common reference to a player digging three or more balls in a row. This term originated on the beach doubles circuit.

Down ball A ball that is hit over the net without much force or from a deep position so that the blockers do not need to jump to attempt a block.

Dump A player—usually the setter—tipping the ball over the net on a team's second, legal contact.

Forearm pass The ball-handling skill in which the ball is contacted on both arms between the area just beyond the wrists and the elbows.

Free ball A ball returned over the net that is easy to handle, usually with either a forearm or overhead technique.

Fronting the hitter A blocking ready position, aligning the blocker directly in front of the attack angle.

Gamelike conditions Any volleyball activity that simulates the tempo, intensity, positions, actions, and player responses of actual, competitive volleyball games.

Goofy footing The opposite footwork of correct steps in a spike approach. For example, a right-handed spiker should approach left, right, left. A goofy-footed right-hander would approach right, left, right.

Half-speed shot An attack hit with topspin but with 50 percent of maximum force of a hard-hit spike. This is also known as a *roll shot*.

Heat seeker Slang for a hard-hit, moving float serve that jams the receiver.

Intermediate contact A necessary and important contact that creates the opportunity to control and terminate a play. Serve receive, setting, and digging are examples.

Invite block   A tactic in which the blockers clearly shift toward one end of the net, obviously showing the opposing setter that they are ignoring a certain hitter or option.

Left-side attacker   The hitter who by choice and rotational design attacks on the left side of the net. This player is also known as the *power* or *strong-side hitter, cannon,* or *ace spiker.*

Matchup   A team strategy in which one team tries to rotate to get certain players across the net from designated opponents to gain attack and/or blocking advantages. A team may also try to start in a rotation that allows a particular server to serve against an opponent's weak receiving pattern.

Multilayered attack   An organizational design for a movement-oriented team attack pattern that designates hitters' routes.

On help   An individual defensive posture in which the player points his or her toes across the court (toward teammates) and twists from the waist up toward the opposing attacker.

Overhead pass   The ball-handling skill in which the ball is contacted on the fingers of both hands that are held above the head. This is also known as an *overhand pass.*

Overlap rule   The designated rotational position each player must be in when the serve is about to be contacted. No player can be in front or behind or to the other side of an *adjacent* player.

Pipe   An attack hit out of the middle of the back row (coined by Chris Marlowe).

Play set   The second option in a multiple-attack system. The play-set hitter often fakes an approach behind the quick hitter and attacks a low, fast set on either side of the quick hitter.

Point of attack   The point at which a hit ball will cross the net.

Point of contact   The exact place on the floor at which the ball becomes playable.

Quick   A short and/or low set that is contacted as the ball is still rising.

Rally-point scoring   A scoring system used in the deciding third or fifth game of a match in which a point is scored on every play regardless who is serving.

RARAR   The acronym for the movement-related keys in ball handling: *R*ead, *A*nticipate, *R*eact, *A*djust, *R*etrieve.

Release set   Every attack pattern should have one player available for a high set in the event that the planned play cannot work. This player is known as the release hitter, and the set he or she receives if necessary is known as a release set.

Right-side attacker   The spiker who attacks primarily from behind the setter on the right side of the net. This player is also known as the *weak-side* or the *play-set hitter.*

Seams   Cracks in the block or defense. The *high seam* is the space between the outside and middle blockers' hands. The *low seam* is a space near the net between the outside and middle blockers' shoulders or arms. The block should fill the spaces between back-row defenders as one would look from the end line toward the net.

Set   The tactical skill of putting the ball above the net so that a teammate can attack it. Although the overhead technique is much preferred, forearm passing and one-handed ball-handling skills can be used to set. Also, a term used internationally to describe a game: A match is composed of three out of five sets.

Shag   The important task of retrieving used balls in a drill and returning them to the bucket. This ensures that there are always balls for the drill and that the area is clear for players.

Side-out   When the team receiving serve wins the rally and gains the right to serve. Unless rally-point scoring is in effect, there is no point scored.

Slide   An attack approach in which a hitter starts on one side of the setter and takes off next to or just beyond the setter and drifts away. There are front slides and backslides.

Small area   The opposite of a big area in serve receive or defense. A player has less geographic responsibility than other teammates.

Stack block   A blocking tactic used against a team that attacks with a quick hitter and a play-set hitter who may hit on either side of the first option. One blocker jumps with the quick hitter and a second blocker lines up behind the first blocker so that he or she can follow the play-set hitter and attempt to block.

Stuff block   The immediate and impactive termination at the net by one or more blockers on an opponent's spike attempt, resulting in the ball landing on the opponent's court in an unplayable fashion. This is also known as a *roof* or *putting a hat on it.*

Swing hitting   The attack pattern in which the hitter starts in the middle of the court and approaches from the right or the left to spike on one side. A conventional approach to an outside set is basically from outside (the court) in toward the point of attack. The swing attack hits the same set but approaches from the inside toward the outside.

Swing offense   A team attack system that uses a multi-layered design and is based on approaches from the inside toward the outside of the court.

Target   The player who is the intended receiver of a previous contact. A serving target is the opposing player who the server selects to serve. The setter is the target who the receiver is trying to pass to.

Team tactics   A game plan that emphasizes a team's strengths and hides its own weaknesses while attacking the opponent's weaknesses.

3-meter line   A line 3 meters away from and running parallel with the net. A back-row attacker must take off from behind this line when hitting.

31X spread   An attack pattern in which the quick hitter approaches for a quick set in net zone 3, the left-side hitter lines up behind the quick hitter and breaks inside or outside as another option, and the right-side hitter approaches net zone 9 for a possible set.

Tipping   An attack in which the hitter fakes a hard swing and, keeping the wrist straight, just touches the ball with stiff fingers and thumb and places it in an open area.

Transition attack   An attack that comes from a dug ball or from a free-ball or down-ball pass during a rally.

'Tweener   A ball that is served or attacked in the area between two serve receivers or defenders.

Vertical   An "in" term for a maximum jump.

X series   Any of a number of attack routes in which one player goes behind another player who is jumping for a quick set. The height for an X play is slightly higher and wider than a quick set and is contacted when the ball is on the way down. This is also known as a *second-tempo set* or a *play set*.

Zone block   A blocking strategy in which the blockers form in balance in front of the attacker, creating an area behind the block in which the ball cannot be forcefully hit.

Index

WORKSHEET 1

Serving

Game Applications

1. Serving is the only skill that is solely _____ by one player.

2. The terminal serve is either an ace or an _____.

3. List three positive outcomes, other than an ace, of a tough serve:

   a. _____

   b. _____

   c. _____

4. The most difficult area to receive serve is _____.

5. List potential serving targets and the rationale behind your choices:

   a. _____

   b. _____

   c. _____

   d. _____

Mechanics

6. Before serving, the first order of business is _____.

7. The three keys to serving are:

   a. _____

   b. _____

   c. _____

8. The key that leads to success or demise is the _____.

9. To improve my serve, I need to: (prioritize needs)

   a. _____

   b. _____

   c. _____

WORKSHEET 2

Forearm Pass

Game Applications

1. Forearm passing is used to:

   a. _____

   b. _____

   c. _____

   d. _____

   e. _____

2. Forearm passing is a(n) intermediate/terminal (choose one) contact. It is performed in a _____ posture range.

Mechanics

3. To execute an effective forearm pass, I must:

   a. _____ at the point of contact *before* the ball.

   b. _____ the incoming ball.

   c. Have my _____ together.

   d. _____ to target.

4. To improve, I need to: (prioritize needs)

   a. _____

   _____

   b. _____

   _____

   c. _____

   _____

WORKSHEET 3

Overhead Pass

Game Applications

1. List three situations calling for an overhead pass:

   a. _____ ,

   b. _____ ,

   c. _____ .

2. What is the most common term and use? _____ .

3. Overhead passing is a(n) intermediate/terminal (choose one) contact.

4. Posture ranges overhead passing is used in what three ranges?

   a. _____

   b. _____

   c. _____

5. Setting is taught and learned in three categories:

   a. _____

   b. _____

   c. _____

6. Every player must be able to accurately back/jump/front/quick/back-row (choose one) set.

Mechanics

7. The learning keys are:

   a. _____

   b. _____

   c. _____

   d. _____

8. To improve, I must: (prioritize needs)

   a. _____

   b. _____

   c. _____

   d. _____

WORKSHEET 4

Attack

Game Applications

1. Individual attack skills include:

   a. _____

   b. _____

   c. _____

   d. _____

2. Team attack is _____.

3. Individual attack shots include:

   a. _____

   b. _____

   c. _____

   d. _____

Mechanics

4. The learning keys are:

   a. Make yourself _____.

   b. *Run* (three-step approach): The key is to _____.

   c. *Jump:* The key is to _____.

   d. *Hit:* The arm is a _____ ; the shoulder is the _____ , the hand is _____.

5. The hand is open/a fist (choose one) when contacting the ball.

6. The ball should be in front of/behind (choose one) the hitting shoulder when hit.

7. To improve, I must: (prioritize needs)

   a. _____

   b. _____

   c. _____

   d. _____

WORKSHEET 5

Block

Game Applications

1. List the three functions of blocking:

   a. _____

   b. _____

   c. _____

2. In beginning volleyball, the most important skill in blocking is knowing _____ .

3. The first and most common blocking system is _____ and _____ .

4. *Match up* means _____ .

5. *Dedicate* means _____ .

6. *Invite* means _____ .

Mechanics

7. List movement/footwork keys:

   a. _____ when moving.

   b. _____ the hitter.

   c. Be _____ and _____ when jumping.

   d. Block sequence: 1. _____ 2. _____ 3. _____ 4. _____

8. List the keys for the hands, arms, and head:

   a. Block _____ and _____ .

   b. _____ and _____ the ball above your head and over the net.

   c. Keep your head _____ and your eyes _____ .

9. To improve, I must: (prioritize needs)

   a. _____

   b. _____

   c. _____

WORKSHEET 6

Floor Defense

Game Applications

1. List the sequence of defense:

    a. _____

    b. _____

    c. _____

    d. _____

2. Floor defense can lead to transitional point-making opportunities. What else does hustling defense do for a team? _____

    _____

Mechanics

3. List the movement skills used in floor defense:

    a. _____

    b. _____

    c. _____

    d. _____

    e. _____

4. List the contact skills:

    a. _____

    b. _____

    c. _____

    d. _____

    e. _____

    f. _____

    g. _____

(continued)

5. List the five general learning keys:

   a. _____

   b. _____

   c. _____

   d. _____

   e. _____

6. To improve, I must: (prioritize needs)

   a. _____

   b. _____

   c. _____

   d. _____